Sweet Treats

FROM BROWNIES TO BRIOCHES

Sweet Treats

FROM BROWNIES TO BRIOCHES

10 INGREDIENTS, 100+ RECIPES

Melodie Asseraf of *Bake it with Mel*

Photography by Amanda Richardson

weldonowen

This book is dedicated to my mom and dad, without whom I would never have known all the flavors and tastes that exist in this world. Thank you for all the beautiful and delicious adventures we've experienced together. And to my grandmother, without whose love, support, and kitchen I would not be here today. You have always been my biggest fan and cheerleader.

CONTENTS

Introduction 8

What You Need 10

The Ten Main Ingredients 12

In a Pinch 14

Chef Mel's Pantry Essentials 15

Build Yourself a Baking Arsenal 16

Basic Baking Techniques 20

The Master Recipes 28

Doughs 101 32

Buttercream 101 46

Small Bites 62

Let's Celebrate 110

Quick Treats 162

Let's Get Technical 204

About the Author 210

Acknowledgments 211

Index 212

INTRODUCTION

Think of me as your butter half and your new kitchen bestie. I'm going to help you level up your baking game and turn you into the best baker you can be! I want you to smile every time you are ready to bake, and, to get there, we've got to build your confidence as a baker. How do we do that? By learning the fundamentals and demystifying the processes that seem overwhelming. A new way to bake with Bake it with Mel!

Being both Parisian and American, I love making sweet treats from both sides of the world. Having had the luxury of eating in the world's finest restaurants and learning recipes from the head pastry chefs at Hôtel Plaza Athénée in Paris, I combine my love for French desserts with simplified techniques and building blocks. So, in this book, you will find recipes for some of my favorites—from the best chocolate chip cookies, fudgy brownies, and birthday cake to brioche, almond galettes, and more sophisticated desserts like soufflés, Paris-Brest, and choux pastries.

Do those French recipes intimidate you? Don't let them! I think baking should be fun, not anxiety-producing. That's why in this book I break down all the culinary techniques I learned in my twenty years as a pastry chef working for the masters of French pastry and show you how to use these building blocks of French pastry for every single recipe you make. Soon you will learn that baking a brioche is just as easy as baking the perfect sugar cookie!

The next thing you'll learn is that you don't have to have a kitchen full of specialty ingredients to make delicious desserts. I'll show you how, with just ten simple ingredients, you cannot only make all of the recipes in this book, but you can also learn exactly how to make cookies to your liking, substitute ingredients without sacrificing flavor, and decipher recipes you read every day to make sure they always turn out the way you want—learning the baker's percentages and having percentages, and having master recipes you can turn into your own.

I know sometimes baking can feel a little like a mystery—how will this recipe work out? What happens if I substitute the milk? Will my creation look as good as the picture? What do I do when my cake fails? Understanding the science behind baking and learning some basic techniques makes all the difference between chaos and success in the kitchen. I've got you covered there, too, with hacks, tips, tricks, troubleshooting, and baking language that will truly make you a more confident baker, not to mention, you'll sound like a pro when you brag to your friends, who will think you went to pastry school.

One note, but a very important one: You may be surprised to see grams listed first in the ingredients lists. This is because the best way to get consistent results every time is to use a scale to measure your ingredients. It's very easy, since you can measure both solids and liquids on the same scale. But, if you don't have a scale, fear not! Volume measurements are given as well (but, really, do yourself a favor and get a scale!).

Whether you are baking brownies for fun on a Saturday afternoon or creating elaborate desserts for an elegant tea party, I am here for you. Life's short, and it's up to you and me to make it sweet.

Sweetly,
Chef Mel

What You Need

From the ten ingredients to your go-to pans, here's everything you need to build your baking arsenal.

The Ten Main Ingredients

Baking is comprised of a lot of the same ingredients, just in different ratios. There are ten main ingredients you should always have on hand; if you have these, you can make just about anything!

Butter

I like European-style butter for baking; its creamier, higher-fat content gives a much nicer golden brown color and flavor profile. Room temperature, cold, and melted butter all produce very different results, so it's important to pay attention to what is required in the recipe. This is crucial when butter is the most important ingredient in your recipe, for instance, for puff pastry.

Sugar

Having fresh sugar that isn't full of humidity or clumps is important in baking, especially when you are making nougats, candy, or caramel, since older sugar will have a tendency to crystallize. The pantry should have granulated, light brown, and powdered sugar.

Eggs

The most important detail about baking with eggs is that they should ALWAYS be at room temperature. Baking with cold eggs will alter the texture and final result of your recipe. I recommend using fresh eggs instead of the ones you buy in a carton. Carton egg whites will not give you the proper volume needed for recipes such as genoise or meringue-based recipes. The average egg usually weighs between 50–55 g (1¾–2 oz) each in the shell. Often, a recipe will call for an uneven amount of egg, such as 120 g (4 oz). To get the remaining amount of egg in the recipe, you'll need to crack one egg into a bowl. Whisk it together and then add the remaining needed from that. This will allow you to have an even distribution of egg white and yolk in the recipe.

Flour and Nut Flour

I use all-purpose flour for pretty much every recipe. Some recipes do call for cake flour or self-rising flour, but all-purpose flour is the one to have in your pantry for the recipes in this book. Nut flour (ground blanched almonds) gives a dense, buttery, and nutty texture in pastries such as financiers, macarons, dacquoise, and flourless chocolate cake. It is also a wonderful ingredient to use in gluten-free recipes. It usually forms a denser crumb and a very moist cake.

Dairy

Whole milk, half-and-half, and heavy cream all have a different fat content and, in general, cannot be substituted for one another where any of them is the main ingredient, so it's best to keep all three on hand, if you can. If you just need to smooth out a batter, however, you can use a small amount of any of them interchangeably.

Yeast

Dry yeast and active dry yeast are the two most common forms of yeast found in the United States. If you can find fresh yeast, always opt for that because it will make for even fluffier bread and a much bigger flavor profile, although fresh yeast is more commonly found in Europe. Check out the Baking Terms section of this book for tips on autolyzing your yeast before baking and to learn more about the bread-making process.

Baking Powder

A very important ingredient, baking powder is made up of baking soda, cream of tartar, and cornstarch and is used to increase volume and lighten the texture of baked goods. You should regularly test the baking powder to make sure it's still good for baking. Simply drop 5g (1 teaspoon) of baking powder into 45ml (3 tablespoons) of boiling hot water; if the baking powder fizzes, it is active and ready to use. This ingredient is active on its own and can be added right to your batter.

Baking Soda

This is another form of leavening and an important ingredient in baking that is used to create a unique, light texture. Baking soda needs to be activated with a liquid and acidic base, so to test whether it is still good, drop 5 g (1 teaspoon) of baking soda into 30 ml (2 tablespoons) of water and 15 ml (1 tablespoon) of lemon juice or vinegar. If it fizzes, it is active and ready to use.

Vanilla

Vanilla comes in all shapes and forms, the most common being extract, beans, powder, and paste. Vanilla bean paste and powder are my favorite ways to use vanilla, as you get a lot of flavor and can see those beautiful vanilla seeds; however, pure vanilla extract is fine as well (be sure to choose pure and not imitation). The most common vanilla beans are the Madagascar, Tahitian, and Mexican vanilla beans. For the softest and largest pods, opt for the Tahitian vanilla bean; although it is the most expensive, it offers an incredible flavor and aroma.

Chocolate

If chocolate is the highlight or star ingredient of your recipe, such as in chocolate mousse or chocolate soufflé, or you will be tempering it, always use high-quality dark chocolate of at least 60 percent cocoa mass. This will create an intense flavor profile and lovely texture. If the chocolate is in chip form, it can easily be substituted for milk chocolate chips in a pinch. In baking, chocolate adds depth of flavor, fat, and texture. Generally, cake batters that use cocoa powder or melted chocolate require additional hydration to keep the batter smooth. Milk chocolate is made with 35 percent to 55 percent cocoa mass. By law, in the US for chocolate to be called milk chocolate it has to contain a minimum of 10 percent cocoa mass; in other countries, milk chocolate must contain a minimum of 25 percent cocoa. This is why milk chocolate from Switzerland, France, and Belgium is so much richer and creamier than US chocolate. In the Basic Baking Techniques chapter, you will find all the best tips on working with chocolate.

In a Pinch

Why these ten ingredients, you may ask? Well, because in a pinch, you can use them very easily as substitutes for other ingredients. You can also make some terrific variations to elevate your baking game.

Butter

These great butter variations can be spread on anything. Store them in a butter bell or wrapped in parchment paper and keep at room temperature so they stay spreadable.

Vanilla butter Mix together 113 g (½ cup) soft butter and 9 g (2 teaspoons) vanilla bean paste or powder mix until well combined.

Almond croissant butter Mix together 113 g (½ cup) soft butter, 20 g (3 tablespoons) powdered sugar, and ½ teaspoon almond extract until smooth.

Whipped butters In a stand mixer, combine 113 g (½ cup) soft butter, 20 g (3 tablespoons) powdered sugar, and 30 g (1½ tablespoons) honey, maple syrup, date syrup, or jam. Whip on medium speed for 10 minutes until fluffy.

Sugar

In a pinch, granulated sugar can be made into just about any kind of sugar. Store these variations in airtight containers at room temperature. Handy tip: add a few marshmallows to the brown sugar jars to keep the sugars soft.

Light brown sugar Place 200 g (1 cup) granulated sugar and 20 g (1 tablespoon) molasses in a food processor and pulse for 3 to 5 minutes, until uniform in color. Allow to sit out on sheet pan for 10 minutes to remove excess moisture.

Dark brown sugar Place 200 g (1 cup) granulated sugar and 40 g (2 tablespoons) molasses in a food processor and pulse for 3 to 5 minutes, until uniform in color. Spread out on a sheet pan and let the mixture dry for 10 minutes to remove excess moisture.

Powdered sugar Place 200 g (1 cup) granulated sugar and 25 g (3 tablespoons) corn starch in a food processor and pulse for 3 to 5 minutes until nice and powdery.

Flour

Most recipes call for all-purpose flour, but for those few recipes that need a variation, there's no need to keep specialty flours on hand! You can make them with all-purpose flour. Store these variations in airtight containers at room temperature.

Self-rising flour For every 120 g (1 cup) of flour, mix in 8 g (1½ teaspoons) baking powder and a pinch of salt. Mix together to distribute the baking powder and salt evenly.

Cake flour For every 120 g (1 cup) flour remove 20 g (2 tablespoons) of flour and add in 20 g (2 tablespoons) of corn starch. Place the ingredients in a sifter and sift together.

Bonus: Nut flour Create any nut flour by toasting the nuts until lightly golden brown to release aromas, allow them to cool completely, then place in a food processor and pulse to the desired texture.

Dairy

Heavy cream is one ingredient to have on hand. You can make all these variations from this one staple ingredient.

Whole Milk Add 120 ml (½ cup) water to 120 ml (½ cup) heavy cream to make 1 cup of whole milk.

Sour cream Combine 240 ml (1 cup) heavy cream and 10 g (2 teaspoons) lemon juice in a jar with a lid. Place the lid on the jar and shake to combine. Add in 60 ml (¼ cup) milk and mix. Remove the lid and cover the opening with cheesecloth or a paper towel and leave at room temperature overnight or up to 24 hours to thicken. Store in the refrigerator for up to 2 weeks.

Crème frâiche Combine 440 ml (2 cups) heavy cream and 45 g (3 tablespoons) cultured buttermilk in a lidded jar. Place the lid on the jar and shake to combine. Remove the lid and cover with cheesecloth or a paper towel and leave at room temperature for 24 hours to thicken. Once thickened, place in the refrigerator and use within 2 weeks.

Butter and buttermilk In a stand mixer, whip heavy cream on high speed until it begins to separate, about 5 minutes. The butter will fall to the bottom of the bowl. The leftover liquid is buttermilk, which you can store in a jar in the refrigerator and use later. Rinse the butter under cold water, then salt or flavor as desired (see Butter). Pat into a bricklike shape, wrap in parchment paper, and store in the refrigerator.

Vanilla

Splurge on high-quality vanilla beans to make these delicious vanilla variations.

Vanilla bean powder After scraping your vanilla beans, wash the pods and dry them well using a paper towel. Place them on a baking sheet and let them dry completely at room temperatur. To dry them quickly, place them in the oven set to the lowest setting (about 200°F [95°C]) for several hours. Once the pods are dry enough to snap when you bend them, place them in a food processor and pulse for 5–7 minutes, until a powder forms. Store at room temperature an airtight container for up to 1 month.

Vanilla extract Take 10 good-quality vanilla beans, slice and scrape 5 beans, and leave 5 beans whole. Place the whole beans, bean pods, and scrapings in a jar with an airtight lid and submerge the pods complete with any 80-proof alcohol (the most commonly used is vodka, as it has a neutral flavor). Screw the lid on tightly and put in a dark place at room temperature for 6–8 months. This is a labor of love, so splurge on nice vanilla beans for the best flavor.

Vanilla sugar Place 200 g (1 cup) granulated sugar and 2 scraped and dried vanilla bean pods in a food processor and pulse for 5 minutes, until you have a uniform powder. If using fresh beans, you can just use the seeds instead of the pods, but they need to be completely dry for best results.

Chef Mel's Pantry Essentials

Here a few more essentials that I always like to keep on hand.

Dry Ingredients

Cornstarch

Cream of tartar

Sprinkles

Chocolate chips (I like Ghirardelli, 60 percent dark chocolate and milk chocolate chips)

Cocoa powder (I like Ghirardelli 100 percent cacao)

Dried coconut

Chestnut puree (crème de marrons)

Fresh Wet Ingredients

Crème fraîche

Buttermilk

Storage

Airtight containers

Plastic wrap

Parchment paper

Build Yourself a Baking Arsenal

Having these basic tools at your disposal will allow you to make just about any dessert. You'll be surprised at what you can do with these few basics.

1. Kitchen scale

2. Metal balloon whisk

3. Heat-resistant rubber spatula

4. Candy thermometer or infrared thermometer

5. Boar-bristle pastry brush (not silicone)

6. Wooden French rolling pin

7. Silicone baking mat

8. 8-inch (20-cm) offset spatula

9. Kitchen scissors

10. Large piping bags (I recommend Matfer piping bags)

11. Paring knife

12. Chef's knife

13. Kitchen timer (I use my cell phone)

14. Peeler (a good one)

15. A zester (I prefer Microplane)

** Stand mixer as a bonus will be your best friend.

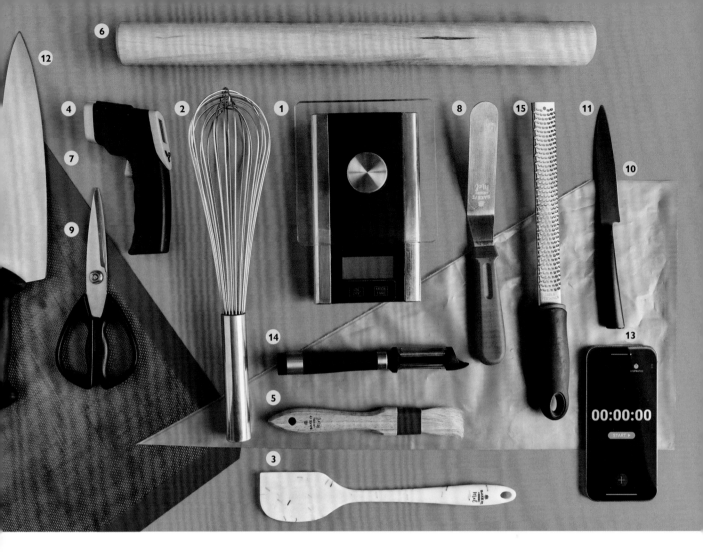

Your Pan Arsenal

These ten pans are essential for your baking arsenal. Be sure to only use metal pans, not silicone, for the best results.

- Half baking sheets (at least four)
- 9-inch (23-cm) round baking pan, 2–3 inches (5–7.5 cm) high
- 6 x 4-inch (15 x 10-cm) round baking pan
- 9-inch (23-cm) square baking pan
- 10-inch (25-cm) round crepe pan
- 9 x 4-inch (23 x 10-cm) loaf pan

- 9 x 13-inch (23 x 33-cm) rectangular pan
- 13 x 18-inch (33 x 46-cm) half baking sheets (at least two)
- 12-compartment muffin tin
- 4-compartment mini loaf pan

Specialty pans I love to keep on hand: madeleine pan, financier pan, tart rings, and entremets rings.

Ten Tips and Tricks to Successful Modern-Day Baking

There is a reason chefs say baking is a science, but it doesn't have to be intimidating or stressful. Baking becomes fun when you control the recipes and, more importantly, the outcome of those recipes. Here are my top ten baking tips to elevate your baking so you can bake like a true pastry chef.

1. DITCH THOSE MEASURING CUPS AND GET A BAKING SCALE

I cannot stress enough how important a baking scale is and how much it will change the way you bake. If you want to have a recipe you can rely on with consistent results, then you need to be able to measure each ingredient accurately. Baking is a science, not a guessing game, so controlling the recipe ensures consistent, perfect results every time. Ingredients have different weights and volumes, so weighing them all in grams is important for the success of a recipe. The scale is not only an important element in preparing the doughs and batters, but also for making sure the cookies and cakes are all uniform in size. Wet ingredients as well as dry can be measured on the scale, as milliliters and grams are the same weight: 240 milliliters of milk is equal to 240 grams of milk.

2. THROW AWAY THOSE SILICONE PANS

If you want professional results and great textures, then you need to bake in metal pans. The heat conduction and distribution is a lot stronger and a lot more even and allows for a perfect golden brown coloring on the outside of baked goods. Silicone pans tend to create the same texture throughout the entire baked good, meaning that the outside, which should be crispy, becomes almost rubbery. Baking in a metal pan will allow for crispy edges and a soft, fluffy center. The only silicone I recommend using is a silicone baking mat, which is used with metal baking pans.

3. PREPARE AND ORGANIZE

Organization in the setup is essential to the success of the recipe. Take the time to read through the full recipe. Measure out all of the ingredients (this is called *mise en place*, meaning "to put in its place"). Preheat the oven. Prepare the baking sheets or cake pans. I promise you this will save you SO much time, frustration, and errors. This will almost guarantee perfection each time you bake. It will also ensure you do not forget certain ingredients.

4. USE ROOM-TEMPERATURE INGREDIENTS

Ingredients such as milk, eggs, and butter combine with a lot more ease when they are at room temperature. To create a creamy batter for cookies or cake layers it is impossible to use cold butter. It simply will not incorporate with the sugar to create a smooth, creamy texture. And cold eggs added into a batter will often cause the batter to separate, which affects the crumb texture in the recipe. I always have butter and eggs out on the counter at room temperature for baking, but if you want to keep these refrigerated, that's fine too. Just be sure to take out the butter 4–5 hours before you start baking, and the other ingredients at least 2 hours before baking. (Also see the section on beurre pommade, which is an even softer form of butter commonly used in French pastries. The texture is similar to that of hand lotion and is very smooth and spreadable.) To bring eggs to room temperature quickly, simply place them in a bowl of warm water for 3–5 minutes.

5. ALWAYS SET THYSELF A TIMER!

It is easy to forget those cookies in the oven if you don't bake often or if you have multiple recipes going at the same time. Set multiple timers so you always have an eye on the baked goods. This will also stop you from opening the oven door preemptively and collapsing certain recipes like genoises, soufflés, fluffy cakes, or pâte à choux. For cookies, I like to set a timer for halfway through the baking process to remind me to rotate the baking sheet.

6. INVEST IN A GOOD STAND MIXER

This is a serious investment in yourself as a baker. It is important to have a good-quality stand mixer to ensure a batter is properly combined, a bread dough is kneaded correctly, or a meringue is whipped enough. Precision in baking ensures success, and you cannot obtain the same level of whipping or combining from a hand mixer.

7. AVOID SUBSTITUTIONS

When it comes to baking, using the correct ingredients has a fundamental effect on the texture and outcome of the baked good. For example, removing eggs reduces the amount of fat, water, and moisture, which then changes the texture of the baked good. Baking is a science, and if you play around with the experiment you will no longer ensure perfect results. So, even though the internet is rife with substitution hacks, do yourself a favor and don't use them when you bake.

8. A SILICONE MAT AND PARCHMENT PAPER ARE YOUR BEST FRIENDS

When baking on a baking sheet, I always use silicone mats for even heat distribution, perfect caramelization, and crispy textures. You can also line the pan with parchment paper, but I only use parchment paper to line a baking or cake pan. No matter which you use, just be sure never to bake directly on a baking sheet without one of these two—baking directly on metal will cause the baked goods to stick, overbake, and become extremely dark on the bottom.

9. USE HIGH-QUALITY INGREDIENTS

High-quality desserts start with high-quality ingredients. Using European-style butter, for example, will give you a much richer flavor, texture, and golden brown finish. Chocolate is also one of the main ingredients you never want to skimp on—a cheap chocolate will give you nothing but trouble in massing, crystallizing, and setting.

If you are putting the work into creating something delicious, then having the best ingredients will make your finished creation that much better.

10. BE GENTLE WHEN BAKING

Every move you make affects the recipe. Use delicate hands to manipulate the doughs and batters. Fold batters gently, and don't overmix. Any time you are folding in flour you are encouraging gluten development, and overmixing or being rough with the dough will create a tough, stretchy texture. Once mixed, let cookie doughs and bread doughs rest before baking to ensure that the gluten has a chance to relax. Take the time to understand how the ingredients come together and how they react to each other so you'll be aware of the desired texture.

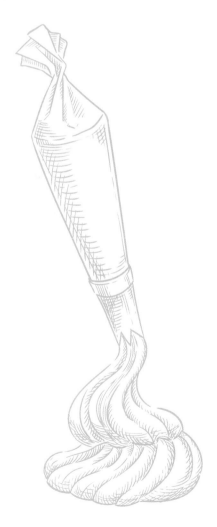

Basic Baking Techniques

For everyday baking like
a French pastry chef

Batter 101

There are two common batter mixing methods; cream butter mixing and liquid fat mixing.

CREAM BUTTER MIXING METHOD

This method is used to incorporate air into the batter by creaming together butter and sugar. It is used in a wide variety of cakes in both French and American pastry traditions—cream butter cakes are leavened by air that is incorporated when the butter and sugar are creamed together, so this step is integral to a cream butter cake's success. This method is done by simply whipping the butter and sugar together (using a stand mixer is best) to obtain a nice homogenous cream. The batter should be fluffy and slightly pale in color, and if you rub a bit between your thumb and finger you should not be able to feel any sugar granules. Cream butter batters are much more stable after mixing. This allows larger batches to be mixed without fear of them falling or not rising when baked, as opposed to egg foam batters, which must be baked right away. You can easily spot this method by simply reading through the ingredients. The order will always be butter, sugar, and eggs, followed by dry ingredients.

LIQUID FAT MIXING METHOD

This technique is also fairly easy to spot in a recipe. The ingredients will start with the dry ingredients and the fat will be either melted butter or oil based. Knowing how to spot this technique can also save you a lot of time in preparing the ingredients, as generally all the dry ingredients will go together and then all of the wet ingredients will go together. This method can consist of either chemical leavening or mechanical leaving or a combination of the two. It is common to overmix this type of recipe to obtain a smooth combined batter, since you have a lot of dry ingredients to combine. A great trick to avoid this issue is to alternate the dry and wet ingredients when mixing to make it easier for the ingredients to combine. These batters tend to be looser and more runny than cream butter batters.

Whole Egg Foam Batters This term specifically refers to the foamy batter of beaten whole eggs or yolks and sugar and is commonly found in recipes such as genoise, flourless chocolate cake, and ladyfingers, where there is no other form of leavening—meaning how well you whip the eggs will determine how fluffy and aerated the cake will be.

How to Get Eggs to Ribbon Stage To get the eggs to ribbon stage, start with room-temperature eggs and whisk them in a stand mixer for 15–20 minutes, until the eggs are pale in color and tripled in volume. To know whether the eggs are at ribbon stage, simply lift up the whisk and as the egg mixture drips down it should form ribbons on the surface of the batter. The ribbon should be thick enough to trace those lines.

Five Rules for Perfect Cookies

1. Use room-temperature, high-quality ingredients, especially butter and chocolate.

2. Let the dough rest in the refrigerator for a few hours before baking.

3. Weigh and roll each cookie into a ball. DO NOT SCOOP. This will give a much nicer texture in the center.

4. Space out the cookies on the baking sheet to give them the best rise and bake.

5. Set a timer and take the cookies out of the oven 2 minutes before you think they are done. Cookies will continue to bake once out of the oven from the residual heat on the baking sheet, and generally you will be left with overbaked cookies if you don't take them out a little early.

How to Butter Pans

There are several ways to butter pans. It always starts with brushing them with a thin layer of soft butter (NOT melted butter). Then add a thin dusting of flour to the pan. If you want to add a little more caramelization and sweetness to the recipe, dust the pan with sugar instead. For chocolate cakes, flourless chocolate cakes, and other chocolate-based batters, consider dusting the pan with cocoa powder instead of flour.

The best way to caramelize puff pastry when making palmiers is to dust the dough with powdered sugar several times throughout the baking process. For perfectly flat, crispy puff pastry sheets, bake them between two baking sheets. The added weight on top of the dough will cause it to stay nice and thin, but still perfectly flaky.

Meringue 101

Meringues are technical and tricky but a very important technique to master. A clean bowl, room-temperature egg whites, and sugar are a must to get this done correctly. There are three types of meringues: French, Italian, and Swiss.

FRENCH MERINGUE

This is the most unstable and delicate type of meringue, but it is the quickest to make and often used for things such as chocolate mousse, soufflés, and flourless chocolate cakes. To make this type of meringue, start by whipping room-temperature egg whites on medium speed. When they appear to be a little frothy, start to add the sugar in increments. NEVER pause the mixer, as you can deflate the egg whites or cause them to become granulated. Once all of the sugar has been incorporated, increase the speed of the mixer to firm up the egg whites into stiff peaks. Once the peaks form around the whisk your meringue is ready to use.

ITALIAN MERINGUE

This is the most commonly used form of meringue, and it is used to make macarons, pavlovas, baked Alaska, and dozens of other desserts. It is very stable and shiny, due to the use of cooked sugar syrup. Use the ratio of twice the amount of sugar to the amount of egg whites as a good benchmark. For best results, always use egg whites at room temperature. A small teaspoon of inverted sugar, such as glucose or corn syrup, can keep the sugar syrup from crystallizing.

To make this meringue, start by whipping the egg whites on low speed. The trick here is to get them nice and frothy as you begin to cook the sugar syrup simultaneously. Place the sugar in a clean saucepan covered with a little water (resembling wet sand consistency) and cook over medium heat. DO NOT STIR OR MIX from this moment forward. Once the sugar begins to boil and most of the water has evaporated,

increase the mixer speed. Continue to let the egg whites whip up while the sugar syrup cooks. Cook the sugar to 250°F (120°C) on a candy thermometer.

Or, to check using ice water, drop the spoon into the sugar syrup and then place it directly into a cup of ice water. If the sugar forms a pliable little ball, it is ready. If the sugar dissolves, cook for a few minutes longer and then test again.

Once the sugar syrup is ready, add it to the egg whites by slowly letting it run down the side of the bowl while the mixer is still running. Stream it in gently to avoid cooking the egg whites. Then mix until the bowl is cold to the touch and the meringue forms shiny, stiff peaks, about 10 minutes (depending on the quantity of meringue you are making). If you are feeling brave, flip the bowl upside down once to test the meringue peaks; they should stay perfectly set.

SWISS MERINGUE

This form of meringue is commonly used for buttercream preparations. In a mixing bowl set over a bain-marie (double boiler), over medium heat, whisk the egg whites and sugar, being careful not to cook the egg whites but simply heat them to 175°F (80°C). The egg whites are ready when you can no longer feel the sugar granules between your fingertips and it is nice and frothy. Once the mixture reaches this stage, set the bowl back on the stand mixer and whip on medium-high speed until stiff peaks form. The bowl should be cool to the touch and the meringue will be shiny and detach itself from the sides of the bowl.

Tips for Making Meringue The number one tip when making any type of meringue is to use aged egg whites. To make aged egg whites, separate whole eggs, put the whites in a jar, and refrigerate for up to 1 week. These make very fluffy meringues.

The worst enemy of meringue is fat. If there is even the smallest amount of yolk in the egg whites you will NEVER be able to whip them to stiff peaks or even soft peaks. Washing the bowl and whisk before getting started, to make sure there is no grease left over from a previous recipe, can save you a lot of aggravation.

The best way to separate the eggs is at room temperature, as the yolk will detach itself from the whites with a lot more ease. Always crack the eggs using separate bowls—don't try to separate them in the mixing bowl, because if you get even a speck of yolk in there you'll have to start all over.

Egg whites are much easier to whip when they are at room temperature. Cold egg whites take much longer to whip and will often produce a grainy texture instead of being shiny and smooth.

Folding Egg Whites When making egg white foams and meringues, folding is as important as beating. After you have beaten the foam to the proper consistency, you must now either fold it into a base or fold other ingredients into it. Folding is very important because it incorporates two preparations into a homogeneous mixture. Do this with a rubber spatula, lifting up the batter from the bottom of the bowl in a circular motion. The key to doing this correctly is to be gentle and delicate.

Bread Dough Techniques

WINDOWPANE TEST

This simple technique is used to test the elasticity of the dough. It tests the gluten development to ensure the bread will be perfectly fluffy. It is a very reliable method used for almost all quick bread recipes, including loafs, dinner rolls, cinnamon rolls, soft pretzels, and more. Before the first proof, simply tear off a piece of dough about the size of golf ball and pull on opposite ends to stretch out the center. The center will become very thin and you'll be able to see light through it, without it tearing right away. This is how you know the dough is ready to be proofed and then baked. If you try to perform this test and the dough rips, knead the dough for longer and test again.

AUTOLYZE

This is the process of testing the yeast before baking. It is always a good idea to test the yeast to ensure that it is active and will produce proper bread. Simply add the yeast to a bowl with 45 ml (3 tablespoons) of warm milk or water and 5 g (1 teaspoon) of sugar. Mix together and let stand for 10 minutes. The yeast mixture should become frothy and thicken. Then add this mixture directly to any recipe you are making. Avoid direct contact with salt, as it can kill the yeast.

Chocolate Tempering 101

Tempering chocolate means melting the chocolate to a certain temperature, so that when it cools it is shiny, smooth, and has a nice snap. It would be impossible for me to teach you everything there is to know about chocolate tempering in one small section, but there is one technique you should learn, as you will use it many times throughout the book: the Seeding Method.

The seeding method is the most efficient, easiest, and most reliable in almost any temperature environment. For this, you will need a bain-marie (double boiler) and a candy thermometer. Separate the chocolate you are using into thirds, then place two-thirds of the chocolate in the bain-marie over medium heat and heat until it is just smooth and liquid, and is in the Heat to Temperature range listed below. Make sure your chocolate does not go over 130°F (55°C)—if you do, the chocolate will scorch. Then slowly add the remaining one-third of the chocolate a few pieces at a time, mixing it in with a spatula to melt (this is the seeding part). The unmelted chocolate will cool the melted chocolate, bringing it into "temper." Take the bowl off the bain-marie (double boiler) and continue stirring and testing the temperature until it gets to the At Temper temperature listed below. Once you're at the desired temperature, spread a bit of chocolate onto a a silicone mat. When it's set, test for the "three Ss"—does it it Snap when you break it, does it have a nice Shine, and is it Smooth, without any lumps? If it meets those criteria, you have perfectly tempered chocolate!

TYPE OF CHOCOLATE	HEAT TO TEMPERATE	AT TEMPER
Dark	113-122°F (45-50°C)	89°F (32°C)
Milk	103-113°F (40-50°C)	88°F (31°C)
White	100-110°F (38-45°C)	86°F (30°C)

One important note: DO NOT try to temper chocolate chips. They have added ingredients that help them keep their shape when they get warm, so they will not melt down smoothly for tempering.

Hint: If you are new to the chocolate world, start with dark chocolate (at least 60 percent cocoa) because it is the easiest chocolate to temper.

A Word About Ingredients

SALTED BUTTER VS. UNSALTED BUTTER

I always recommend using unsalted butter in baking to retain control of the recipe. Different butter brands contain different salt amounts, and to ensure the same consistency throughout, it is safer to use unsalted butter and add the amount of salt called for in the recipe.

FRESH EGGS VS. CARTON EGGS

I recommend only using fresh eggs in recipes. The process of preserving eggs you get in cartons makes them different from fresh eggs, and you will never obtain the same result in baked goods if you use carton eggs. You cannot whip carton egg whites into meringues or egg yolks into pâte à bomb with the best results. Fresh eggs are always the number one choice for baking.

FRESH VS. FROZEN FRUITS

I never recommend using frozen fruits if you have the possibility of using fresh ones. Frozen fruits have much less flavor and a lot of added water. This water often denatures the dough or batter it is incorporated into. Use fresh fruits dusted with a small of amount of cornstarch to keep them from sinking to the bottom of the dessert. This also allows you to control the sweetness, tartness, and all flavor aspects of the dessert more closely.

The Master Recipes

Classic French pastry is made up of building block recipes that are then used to create other desserts. These are the essential recipes to master to enable you to make hundreds of creations. If you learn how to make pastry cream and pâte à choux, for example, you are now set up to make dozens of choux desserts, such as the Paris-Brest, cream-filled choux, religieuses, éclairs, and the famous croquembouche, to name a few. Mastering these fundamental techniques and recipes will give you the freedom to write your own recipes and create your own desserts with elegance and amazing flavor combinations. French pastry doesn't have to be overwhelming or intimidating; these basic recipes will help you understand the science behind baking and build yourself an arsenal of reliable fundamental recipes.

Genoise

Genoise is a classic spongy cake layer, and it's great for stacking cakes together. It's used in several other desserts in this book. The delicate texture comes from beating the eggs to ribbon stage, which is the key to a nice soft crumb. This cake also freezes well and is wonderful for assembling last-minute desserts.

Yield: One 6-inch (215-cm) cake

Prep Time: 20 minutes

Bake Time: 25 minutes

Difficulty: Intermediate

Tools: Balloon whisk, 6-inch (15-cm) cake pan

200 g (4) eggs, at room temperature

135 g (⅔ cup) granulated sugar

120 g (1 cup) all-purpose flour

40 ml (3 tablespoons) whole milk

Chef Tips

Use eggs at room temperature for this recipe. It will significantly shorten the amount of time you will need to whip the eggs. This recipe uses mechanical leavening only, which means all the height of the cake will come from how well you whip the eggs, so take your time whipping those eggs. It will make for an egg-celent fluffy genoise.

1. Preheat the oven to 350°F (175°C). Brush a round 6-inch (15-cm) cake pan with butter and dust with flour. Line the bottom and sides of the pan with parchment paper.

2. In a stand mixer fitted with a whisk attachment or with a hand mixer, add the eggs and half of the sugar. Whisk immediately (letting the sugar sit on the yolks can cook them) on medium speed until doubled in volume, about 10 minutes. Add the remaining sugar and whisk until tripled in volume and the mixture is at the ribbon stage (page 22), about 10 minutes longer. The mixture should be very fluffy, pale in color, and hold its shape. If it is not quite thick enough, whip the eggs for an additional 10 minutes.

3. Using a balloon whisk, gently fold in the flour (using a rubber spatula or the stand mixer can cause flour pockets in the batter and deflate the eggs). Alternate between adding in a little bit of flour and 15 ml (1 tablespoon) of milk at a time. Use the whisk to lift the egg mixture so the flour gets incorporated.

4. Pour the batter into the prepared pan and immediately place in the oven. Bake for 20 minutes (do not open the oven during this time). At 20 minutes, insert a toothpick into the center of the cake. It should come out clean; if not, continue baking for 5 minutes.

5. Let the cake cool for 10 minutes before unmolding it. Store in an airtight container for up to 1 week at room temperature, or place between cake boards, wrap in plastic wrap, and store in the freezer for up to 1 month.

Variations

Swap 25 g (1 oz) of cocoa powder for 25 g (1 oz) of the flour for a chocolate version.

Hazelnut Dacquoise Cake

Dacquoise is a spongy cake layer made up egg whites, ground nuts, and sugar. It is a staple for a lot of French cake recipes because it is wonderful to layer with different creams and mousses and can be used in various entremets. It also freezes very well. It has a flavor and texture that is similar to homemade ladyfingers, but is a bit more delicate. The hazelnut is my favorite, and it won me the best dessert on the show *Chopped*.

Yield: Two 9-inch (23-cm) cake layers

Prep Time: 10 minutes

Bake Time: 20 minutes

Difficulty: Intermediate

Tools: Stand mixer, piping bag, round piping tip, silicone mat

100 g (1 cup) powdered sugar

100 g (1 cup) hazelnut flour (powdered hazelnuts)

120 g (4) egg whites, at room temperature

45 g (3 tablespoons) granulated sugar

50 g (⅓ cup) chopped hazelnuts

1. Preheat the oven to 350°F (175°C). Line a baking sheet with a silicone mat or parchment paper.

2. In a mixing bowl, add the powdered sugar and hazelnut flour and whisk to combine.

3. In a stand mixer, add the room-temperature egg whites and granulated sugar. Whisk until stiff peaks form. The mixture will be nice and shiny and hold its shape on the end of the whisk and pull away from the sides of the bowl when ready. Fold the meringue into the hazelnut flour mixture using a rubber spatula, being gentle so as not to deflate the egg whites. Load this mixture into a piping bag fitted with a round piping tip.

4. Pipe out two 9-inch (23-cm) disks on the prepared baking sheet. Sprinkle the tops of the cakes with the chopped hazelnuts.

5. Bake right away for 20 minutes, or until fully golden brown. Let cool completely on the baking sheet. Once cooled, use in a recipe or wrap in plastic wrap between cake boards and store in the freezer for up to 1 month.

Variations

- Try using pistachio or almond flour as a delicious alternative.

- If you don't want to pipe, simply pour the batter onto a half sheet baking pan, prepared as above, and smooth out the batter evenly with an offset spatula. Once cooled, you can use cookie cutters or cake rings to cut out your layers. Store these the same way as above.

Doughs 101

These doughs are the building blocks that will allow you to create hundreds of different desserts, including several in this book. Each dough utilizes a different technique that produces a unique texture.

Sweet Pastry Dough
(Pâte Sucrée)

This is one of the most fundamental doughs in French baking. Pâte sucrée (French for sweet dough) can be used for so many preparations, but most commonly for pies and fruit tarts. This a flaky shortcrust pastry made of eggs, butter, flour, and sugar. It comes together quickly and is great to keep in the freezer for so many different quick desserts.

Yield: 500 g (18 oz) dough
Prep Time: 10 minutes
Rest Time: 2 hours
Difficulty: Easy
Tools: Stand mixer, rolling pin, rubber spatula

120 g (½ cup + 1 tablespoon) unsalted butter, at room temperature

80 g (¾ cup) powdered sugar

50 g (1) egg, at room temperature

220 g (1¾ cups) all-purpose flour

30 g (5 tablespoons) almond flour

1. In a mixing bowl fitted with a paddle attachment, or by hand using a spatula, add the butter and sugar. Cream together on medium speed for 2–3 minutes until smooth and creamy.

2. Add the egg and mix on high speed to combine. Scrape down the sides of the bowl and add the all-purpose and almond flours. Mix on medium speed for 1 minute until the dough comes together. Finish combining the dough by hand to prevent overmixing.

3. Form the dough into a rectangular bricklike shape (called a "paton") and wrap it in plastic wrap. Store in the refrigerator for at least 2 hours to allow the flavors to come together and to relax the gluten. When ready to use, divide the paton in half, place between two pieces of parchment paper, and roll out according to the recipe. The dough can be stored, either as a paton or rolled out, in an airtight container or wrapped in plastic wrap, in the refrigerator for up to 5 days, or freeze for up to 1 month.

Rough Puff Pastry
(Pâte Feuilletée Rapide)

Making classic puff pastry is a long and difficult process to master. It requires several hours to form the dough, roll it out, and complete the turns, and the process can often be discouraging for novice bakers. This quick rough puff pastry delivers all the flakiness in half the time. Using small pieces of cold butter rather than incorporating the butter as one slab makes this process easy and seamless. You can use this for many recipes, including viennoiseries, breakfast pastries, palmiers, millefeuilles, and so many more you'll also find throughout this book.

Yield: 2 full sheets puff pastry, about 300 g (11 oz) each

Prep Time: 15 minutes

Rest Time: 30 minutes in between each turn (6 double turns)

Difficulty: Intermediate

Tools: Stand mixer, rolling pin, pastry brush, silicone mat

150 g (¾ cup) granulated sugar

240 g (2 cups) all-purpose flour

65 g (4 tablespoons) unsalted butter, at room temperature

15 g (1 tablespoon) granulated sugar

Pinch of salt

100–110 ml (½ cup) ice water

150 g (5.4 oz) cold unsalted butter, cubed

1. In the mixing bowl of the stand mixer fitted with paddle attachment, add the 240 g (2 cups) flour, room-temperature butter, sugar, and salt. Mix together. Stream in the ice water as you mix on medium speed to form the "*detrampe*" dough. Add the water slowly; you may not need all of it. The dough should hold its shape but not be wet. Add the cold cubed butter. DO NOT work it into the dough. You want to see all of those cubes visible in the dough. Simply pulse the mixer once or twice or shape by hand. The butter will create those flaky layers as you complete the different turns.

2. Line the workstation with a long piece of plastic wrap. Place the dough in the center and shape it into a paton, a flat bricklike shape. Wrap and refrigerate for 1 hour. Leave the work surface prepped with the rolling pin and dusted with flour.

3. Complete two double turns (see the diagram on the right). Roll the dough lengthwise into a long rectangle roughly 14 inches (35.5 cm) long by 6 inches (15 cm) wide. Apply even pressure to roll the dough out as evenly as you can. Dust with flour often to prevent sticking. Always keep the rolled-in edge on the left and roll out the same way each time. Refrigerate for 1 hour.

- Make sure to use ice water and not room-temperature water.
- Keep dusting the rolling pin and work surface with flour as you complete the six double turns to keep the butter from sticking to the counter. If the dough starts sticking too much, refrigerate it for 30 minutes and then complete another turn.
- The dough can be affected by humidity, weather, altitude, and many other factors. Listen to the dough; you may need to do this on a different day.
- Dusting puff pastry with a little powdered sugar will also help with caramelization and nice even coloring.

4. Repeat the process three more times to complete six double turns, refrigerating after every two turns for 30 minutes.

5. When ready to use the dough, cut it in half horizontally across the paton. Each half will create one full puff pastry rectangle.

6. To freeze the dough, roll it out between two sheets of parchment paper and keep the dough on a baking sheet.

7. When ready to bake, preheat the oven to 350°F (175°C). Bake according to the recipe until golden brown.

French Brioche Dough

The French brioche as we know it was created in Normandy around the sixteenth century. The word *brioche* comes from the verb *brier*, meaning "to grind," as the traditional way of making this bread involved beating the dough with large wooden pins to incorporate the butter. This light, fluffy bread is perfect for everything from breakfast breads to burger buns to French toast. It's an iconic recipe that will elevate your bread, making each bite irresistible.

Yield: 12 brioches of 60 g (2 oz) each

Prep Time: 30 minutes

Rest Time: 2½ hours

Bake Time: 20 minutes

Difficulty: Intermediate

Tools Stand mixer, pastry brush, bench scraper

For the Dough

7 g (2 teaspoons) active dry yeast

45 ml (3 tablespoons) water

45 g (3 tablespoons) granulated sugar

320 g (2⅔ cups) all-purpose flour, plus more for dusting

200 g (4) whole eggs

170 g (¾ cup) soft unsalted butter

For the Egg Wash

50 g (1) whole egg

20 g (1) egg yolk

30 ml (2 tablespoons) heavy cream

For the Decoration

100 g (3½ oz) pearl sugar crystals

1. Line a baking sheet with a silicone mat or parchment paper.

2. To make the dough: In a small bowl, combine the yeast, water, and half of the sugar and let sit for 10 minutes until frothy (see page 25 for more on autolyzing yeast).

3. In the bowl of a stand mixer fitted with the hook attachment, combine the flour, remaining sugar, eggs, and yeast mixture. Knead on medium speed until the dough is smooth and pulls away from the sides of the bowl, about 10 minutes.

4. Continue to mix on medium speed as you add in the butter 1 tablespoon at a time. The butter should be soft and spreadable. Once all of the butter has been added, mix on high speed for 2 minutes to create a dough that's very smooth, soft, and shiny. Perform the window pane test to ensure the bread will be perfectly fluffy (page 25).

5. Turn the dough onto a lightly floured work surface and form into a large ball. Place in a greased bowl and proof in a warm place until doubled in size, about 1 hour.

6. Turn the dough onto the work surface and press down to release any gas. Cut the dough into 12 equal pieces of 60 g (2 oz) each using a bench scraper. Roll each piece into a nice round ball and place them on the prepared baking sheet. Proof in a warm spot until doubled in size, 1–1½ hours.

7. Preheat the oven to 350°F (175°C).

8. To make the egg wash: In a small bowl, add the egg, egg yolk, and heavy cream and stir until smooth. Brush each brioche with the egg wash and sprinkle with the pearl sugar.

9. Bake for 20 minutes, until each brioche is golden brown on the top and bottom.

10. Store an airtight bag for up 3 days. Keep frozen for up to 3 weeks.

11. Warm frozen brioche in a 300°F (150°C) oven for 5 minutes.

Easy Flaky Crust
(Pâte Sablée)

This lightly sweetened dough is also perfect for all sorts of savory recipes and is one of the building blocks in French pastry. The main difference between pâte sucrée and pâte sablée is that the first uses the cream butter method to create a smooth, creamy texture before adding in the rest of the ingredients. Pâte sablée is made by rubbing the cold butter into the flour and dry ingredients to create a "sable," or sandlike texture, initially. Once combined with other ingredients, it creates a smooth dough often used for tarts and petits fours. Pâte sablée is not to be confused with pâte brisée, which is much more flaky and less crumbly, and most commonly used for quiches.

Yield: 607 g (21.7 oz) dough
Prep Time: 20 minutes
Rest Time: 3 hours
Difficulty: Easy
Tools: Rolling pin, stand mixer, silicone mat

290 g (2½ cups) all-purpose flour

60 g (⅓ cup) granulated sugar

227 g (1 cup) cold unsalted butter, cubed

40 g (2) egg yolks, at room temperature

Chef Tips

- Work the dough as little as possible. You can easily overmix it. Pulse the mixer to combine the ingredients and finish the dough by hand for the best results.

- If the dough is sticky, roll it out between two sheets of parchment paper and refrigerate until firm. Remove the top parchment and flip the dough right into the pan.

- The dough can be refrigerated for up 2 weeks or frozen for up to 1 month.

1. In the bowl of a stand mixer or by hand, mix together the flour and sugar. Add the cold cubed butter and mix on medium speed for 2–3 minutes until the dough starts coming together. Add the egg yolks and mix for 1 minute. Scrape down the sides of the bowl and mix for 1 minute longer so everything is nice and combined.

2. Roll out plastic wrap on the work surface and place the dough in the center. Form it into a paton (rectangular bricklike shape) and cover. Refrigerate for 2–3 hours before rolling it out.

3. When ready to use, roll out onto a lightly floured work surface or on a sheet of parchment paper.

4. If you are using this dough for tart shells, hand pies, pies, or pot pies, brush with egg wash (page 35) before baking at 350°F (175°C) for a nice, golden brown color.

Quiche Dough *(Pâte Brisée)*

Crisp, buttery, and tender, this dough is so delicious. It comes together easily and has
a very flaky texture. It barely has any sugar, so it is wonderful to use for savory recipes.
This dough is usually used for quiches and very flaky tart shells. Its name, pâte brisée, pronounced
"pat bri-zay," means "broken or shattered dough" in French and refers to its flaky texture.
This recipe is also one of the fundamental French dough recipes.

Yield: 480 g (17 oz) dough

Prep Time: 15 minutes

Rest Time: 2–3 hours

Difficulty: Easy

Tools: Rolling pin, stand mixer

240 g (2 cups) all-purpose flour

15 g (1 tablespoon) granulated
sugar

128 g (½ cup + 1 tablespoon)
cold unsalted butter, cubed

40 g (2) egg yolks, at room
temperature

60 ml (¼ cup) ice water

Chef Tips

- Work the dough as little as
  possible. You can easily overmix
  it. Pulse the mixer to combine
  the ingredients and finish the
  dough by hand for the best
  results. Be sure to use ice water
  to combine this dough. Keeping
  the butter cold is what creates
  those flaky layers in the dough.
  Prepare this dough in advance
  and roll it out when ready
  to bake.

- If the dough is sticky, roll it out
  between two sheets of parchment
  paper and refrigerate until firm.
  Remove the top parchment and
  flip the dough right into the pan.

- The dough can be refrigerated
  for up 2 weeks or frozen for up
  to 1 month.

1. In the bowl of a stand mixer or by hand, combine the flour
and sugar. Add the cold butter and mix on medium speed for
2–3 minutes, for the dough to start coming together. Add
the egg yolks and mix for 1 minute. Scrape down the sides
of the bowl and stream in the ice water slowly as you mix on
medium speed to bring the dough together.

2. Place a piece of plastic wrap on the work surface and place
the dough in the center. Form it into a paton (rectangular
bricklike shape) and cover. Refrigerate for 2–3 hours before
rolling it out.

3. When ready to use, divide the dough in half and roll out to
¼ inch (6 mm) thick on a lightly floured countertop or on a
sheet of parchment paper.

4. If you are using this dough for tart shells, hand pies, pies,
pot pies, or quiches, brush with egg wash (page 35) before
baking at 350°F (175°C) for a nice golden brown color.

Pâte à Choux Dough

Welcome to another iconic recipe in French pastry. Pâte à choux is a very important building block; once you master this recipe, you'll be able to make more than a dozen desserts that use pâte à choux, such as religieuses, éclairs, choux puffs, St. Honoré, and profiteroles, to name a few. Although now a staple in French pastry, this dough's origins are actually Italian and date back to the sixteenth century. Its name has changed over the years from "pâte à chaud" to "pâte à choux."

Yield: 20–25 choux puffs

Prep Time: 10 minutes

Bake Time: 20–25 minutes

Difficulty: Intermediate

Tools: Stand mixer, saucepan, silicone mat, pastry brush, piping bag, rolling pin

---

120 ml (½ cup) whole milk

60 g (¼ cup) unsalted butter, cubed

30 g (2 tablespoons) granulated sugar

Pinch of salt

100 g (¾ cup) all-purpose flour

150–200 g (3 to 4) eggs, at room temperature

For the Egg Wash (if not making the craquelin layer)

50 g (1) egg

15 ml (1 tablespoon) heavy cream or milk

For the Craquelin Layer

50 g (¼ cup) unsalted butter, at room temperature

60 g (¼ cup) raw sugar

60 g (½ cup) all-purpose flour

1. Preheat the oven to 350°F (175°C). Line two baking sheets with silicone mats or parchment paper. Fit a piping bag with a round tip (or no tip, if you don't have one).

2. In a 3- or 4-qt (2.7- or 3.6-L) saucepan, add the milk, cubed butter, granulated sugar, and salt. Bring to a simmer over medium heat, and mix once or twice as you heat it so the sugar dissolves and doesn't stick to the bottom of the pot.

3. When the milk mixture comes to a full simmer, add the flour all at once. Using a wooden or rubber spatula, stir to form the dough. This is called the "panade." Dehydrating the dough during this process is key, so continue to stir until a film or skin appears on the bottom of the pot; for 5–7 minutes.

4. Transfer the dough to a stand mixer fitted with a paddle attachment. Mix for 2–3 minutes to release all of the steam. This is important to not curdle the eggs. Once the bowl feels cool to the touch, add the eggs one at a time. The humidity in the air and how much you dehydrated the dough will determine whether you need 4 or 5 eggs. You should obtain a thick, smooth, and glossy dough. To know you have added enough eggs, lift up the paddle; the dough should fall slowly into the bowl, forming a ribbon thick enough to hold it shape (page 22).

5. Load the dough into the prepared piping bag and pipe the choux as evenly as possible onto the prepared baking sheet in the shape directed by the recipe. You can do a stick shape, a puff, or a swirl. Count in your head to a set rhythm for consistent piping: 1-2-3, 1-2-3 . . . . Space the choux out on the baking sheet and do not pipe them in a straight line, so there is no risk of them touching as they bake.

6. If you are not making the craquelin layer, make the egg wash by whisking the egg and heavy cream in a small bowl. (If making the craquelin layer, skip to step 7.) Using a pastry brush, delicately brush a small amount of egg wash on each pastry, being careful not to press too hard and deform the choux.

7. For that extra pro touch, make the craquelin layer (optional). There is no need for the egg wash with this technique. In a small bowl, combine the room-temperature butter, raw sugar, and flour and mix with a rubber spatula for 2 minutes.

8. Roll out the craquelin dough between two sheets of parchment paper to prevent it from sticking to the rolling pin. It should be a little less than ¼ inch (6 mm). Place the sheet of dough on a baking sheet and put in the refrigerator for 20–60 minutes. Once the dough is nice and firm, remove it from the refrigerator and gently peel off the top parchment paper.

9. Using a round cookie cutter about the same diameter as the choux puff, cut out circles of the craquelin dough. Place one circle on top of each choux. When this bakes the crunchy top layer will help the steam distribute evenly, creating a much rounder and more perfect choux puff. (You can make these sheets in advance and store them in the freezer between two sheets of parchment paper for several weeks. Use immediately after removing them from the freezer.)

10. Place the baking sheets one at time in the oven and bake them separately (not one on top of the other). DO NOT OPEN THE OVEN for the first 15 minutes. Allow the choux puffs to rise completely before checking on them to see if they need additional baking time to reach the optimal color. They should be perfectly golden brown and puffy. The choux are baked through when doubled in size and a dark golden brown all over. When you lift one off the baking sheet, it should also be golden brown on the bottom. Allow them to cool completely—successful pâte à choux will be completely hollow in the center once cooled.

11. You can store baked pâte à choux in the freezer in airtight bags for up to 1 month.

12. When ready to use, remove them from the freezer and let them come to room temperature. If they are a little soft, place them in the oven on a baking sheet at 350°F (175°C) for 5 minutes. This will dry out any excess moisture in the dough.

13. Fill with your favorite cream or mousse and serve right away, or try your hand at one of the other recipes in the book that uses pâte à choux.

Basic Soft and Chewy Sugar Cookies

I think it's important to have a great sugar cookie dough that is reliable,
comes together quickly, and can be baked within a few minutes.

Yield: 16 cookies of 40 g
(1½ oz) each

Prep Time: 20 minutes

Bake Time: 15 minutes

Difficulty: Easy

Tools: Stand mixer, silicone mat

---

113 g (½ cup) unsalted butter,
at room temperature

110 g (1 cup) powdered sugar

110 g (½ cup) granulated sugar,
plus more for rolling

50 g (1) egg, at room temperature

240 g (2 cups) all-purpose flour

10 g (2 teaspoons) baking powder

5 g (1 teaspoon) baking soda

Chef Tips

*To store the uncooked dough,
flatten it into a rectangle and
wrap with plastic wrap. Store in the
refrigerator for up to 2 weeks or in
the freezer for up to 1 month.*

1. Preheat the oven to 350°F (175°C). Line a baking sheet with
a silicone mat or parchment paper.

2. In a stand mixer fitted with a paddle attachment or by hand,
add the butter and both sugars. Mix together on medium speed
for 5–7 minutes until light and creamy.

3. Scrape down the sides of the bowl, add the egg, and mix for
an additional 2–3 minutes until smooth and combined.

4. Add the flour, baking powder, and baking soda and mix on
low speed for 1–2 minutes, just to bring the dough together. You
can finish forming the dough by hand to avoid overmixing.

5. Weigh out the cookie dough on a baking scale so each
piece weighs the same amount. I like to go with 40 g (1½ oz).
Once all of the dough is weighed, roll each piece into a perfect
round ball.

6. Pour some granulated sugar into a bowl or shallow plate.
Roll each ball in the sugar and place on the prepared baking
sheet, spacing them out evenly for better airflow. Bake for
about 15 minutes. The tops of the cookies will be soft but the
edges will be lightly golden brown. Let the cookies cool to
room temperature before moving them.

7. Store an airtight container at room temperature for up to
1 week.

Basic Brown Sugar Cookie Dough

Think of this cookie dough as a blank canvas for any type of cookie you have ever wanted to make. It is the perfect chewy cookie that you can add any toppings to. You can easily make over fifty different types of cookies with this base. You can also divide the cookie dough to make different flavors with one batch. It is very important to use the ingredients at room temperature for the best results. Try to use a European-style butter for more depth of flavor and a richer color.

Yield: About 900 g (32 oz), 18–20 cookies of 50 g (1¾ oz) each

Prep Time: 20 minutes

Rest Time: 6–12 hours

Bake Time: 12 minutes

Difficulty: Easy

Tools: Rubber spatula, baking sheet, baking mat, stand mixer

227 g (1 cup) unsalted butter, at room temperature

220 g (1 cup) light brown sugar

100 g (2) eggs, at room temperature

380 g (3⅛ cups) all-purpose flour

30 g (¼ cup) cornstarch

15 g (2½ teaspoons) baking powder

300 g (10.7 oz) chocolate chips, nuts, or any additions you like

1. In a mixing bowl fitted with a paddle attachment or by hand, add the butter and brown sugar and mix on medium speed for about 5 minutes. Scrape down the sides of the bowl and mix for 1 minute longer.

2. Add the eggs one at time, mixing in between each egg for 2 minutes until smooth.

3. Add the flour, cornstarch, and baking powder and mix on low speed just until the dough comes together. Do not overmix or the dough will become sticky. Add the chocolate chips and gently mix to combine.

4. Wrap the dough in plastic wrap and let it rest in the refrigerator for at least 6 hours, up to overnight.

5. When ready to bake, preheat the oven to 350°F (175°C). Line a baking sheet with a silicone mat or parchment paper.

6. Roll each cookie into a 50-g (1¾oz) ball. Space them out on the baking sheet for better airflow when baking. Bake for 10–12 minutes. The top of the cookie should still appear slightly gooey and soft. The edges will be golden brown.

7. Remove from the oven and gently slide the silicone mat off the baking sheet to allow to cool on the counter and stop the baking process. Do not attempt to remove the cookies individually, because they will break.

Crème Anglaise for Sauce

This beautiful cream made its first appearance in the royal court in England in the sixteenth century, which is where it gets its name, crème anglaise (English cream). It has since been modified and adapted in many different countries. In French pastry, this sauce often accompanies a chocolate-based dessert like a soufflé or flourless chocolate cake. The quality of the vanilla really matters here for great flavor.

Yield: 634 ml (about 2¾ cups)

Prep Time: 10 minutes

Cook Time: 8 minutes

Difficulty: Intermediate

Tools: Rubber spatula, saucepan, paring knife

235 ml (1 cup) whole milk

235 ml (1 cup) heavy cream

8 g (2 teaspoons) vanilla bean paste or 2 vanilla beans, split and scraped

80 g (⅓ cup) granulated sugar

80 g (4) egg yolks, at room temperature

1. In a 3- or 4-qt (2.7- or 3.6-l) saucepan, add the milk, cream, vanilla paste or seeds, and half the sugar. Bring to a boil over high heat and stir occasionally to make sure the sugar is properly dissolved.

2. In a small bowl, combine the egg yolks and remaining sugar. Whisk together until pale in color, just 2 minutes.

3. To temper the egg yolk mixture, pour a small amount of the hot milk over the egg yolks and whisk together. Pour the mixture back into the saucepan and cook over low heat. Patience is key, as the crème anglaise can never boil. Cook the yolk mixture low and slow until it coats the back of a wooden spoon. When you trace a line with your finger through it on the back of the spoon, it should leave a clean line. This technique is called "nappage."

4. Immediately pour the crème into an airtight container. Let cool at room temperature, but cover the top with a lid or plastic wrap to prevent a skin from forming on the top. Store in the refrigerator for up to 1 week.

Crème Anglaise Ice Cream Base

It's important to have a reliable ice cream base recipe that you can turn into any flavor you want. This vanilla-based ice cream works wonderfully with any ingredients you want to add (just make sure to maintain the same ratio of liquid to solid). Perfectly rich, creamy, and decadent, this ice cream is one of my favorites.

Yield: 1 l (about 4 cups)

Prep Time: 20 minutes

Cook Time: 10 minutes

Difficulty: Intermediate

Tools: Rubber spatula, saucepan, paring knife

500 ml (2⅛ cups) heavy cream

235 ml (1 cup) whole milk

8 g (2 teaspoons) vanilla bean paste or 2 vanilla beans, split and scraped

200 g (1 cup) granulated sugar

100 g (5) egg yolks, at room temperature

1. In a 3- or 4-qt (2.7- or 3.6-l) saucepan, add the cream, milk, vanilla paste or seeds, and half the sugar. Bring to a boil over high heat and stir occasionally with a rubber spatula to make sure the sugar is properly dissolved.

2. In a small bowl, add the egg yolks and remaining sugar. Whisk together until pale in color, just 2 minutes.

3. To temper the egg yolk mixture, pour a small amount of the hot milk over the egg yolks and whisk together. Pour the mixture back into the saucepan and cook over low heat. Patience is key, as the crème anglaise can never boil. Cook the yolk mixture low and slow until it coats the back of a wooden spoon. When you trace a line with your finger through it on the back of the spoon, it should leave a clean line. This technique is called "nappage."

4. Immediately pour the ice cream base into airtight container. Let cool at room temperature and then keep in the refrigerator. When ready to make ice cream, simply pour the mixture into the ice cream machine and churn according to the manufacturer's directions. You can add 100 g (3½ oz) of anything you want, such as chocolate spread, fresh fruits, candied nuts, or caramel sauce.

5. Keep in the freezer for up to 2 weeks. You can keep the ice cream base for up to 1 week in the refrigerator before churning it.

Pastry Cream

Pastry cream is a custard that is made on the stovetop. It is a little complex to master to get just the right thickness without curdling the eggs. If you walk into a patisserie in Paris, everything from flan to fruit tarts to viennoiseries uses a variation of this beautifully smooth pastry cream. This recipe is very reliable, so you can make many different flavors once you've got the technique down.

Yield: 400 g (14 oz)
Prep Time: 20 minutes
Cook Time: 15 minutes
Chill Time: 12 hours
Difficulty: Intermediate
Tools: Balloon whisk

265 ml (1⅛ cups) whole milk

65 g (⅓ cup) granulated sugar

4 g (1 teaspoon) vanilla bean paste or 1 vanilla bean, split and scraped

50 g (1) egg, at room temperature

25 g (¼ cup) all-purpose flour

1. In a 3- or 4-qt (2.7- or 3.6-L) saucepan, add the milk, half the sugar, and the vanilla paste or seeds. Bring to a high simmer over low heat and stir with a whisk to help dissolve the sugar.

2. In a mixing bowl, add the egg, remaining sugar, and flour. Whisk to combine.

3. Temper the egg mixture by pouring a small amount of warm milk into the eggs and whisking well. Pour the egg mixture back into the milk mixture in the saucepan. This is important to avoid curdling the eggs.

4. Raise the heat to medium. Once you spot the first bubble, set a timer for 3 minutes and do not stop whisking. This will ensure you cook the pastry cream enough so it is safe to eat and will be firm enough to use.

5. Line a baking sheet with plastic wrap to have ready for when the pastry cream is cooked. Pour the pastry cream directly onto the plastic wrap and cover it with more plastic wrap to prevent the air from creating a "skin" on top of the cream. Allow the cream to chill overnight for 12 hours before using it in a recipe.

6. Keep in the refrigerator for up to 1 week. Do not freeze.

Variations
- To make chocolate pastry cream, add 50 g (1¾ oz) of dark chocolate chips to the hot pastry cream.
- You can add praline paste or different extracts.

Crème Légère

Crème légère is a combination of equal parts pastry cream and whipped cream. It has a great depth of flavor and is wonderful to pipe on pretty much anything because it looks beautiful and holds its shape very well. If you add a sheet of bloomed gelatin, it is called diplomat cream, which has a more stable base for larger cakes and entremets.

Yield: About 500 ml (2⅛ cups)

Prep Time: 30 minutes

Difficulty: Intermediate

Tools: Stand mixer, balloon whisk, rubber spatula, piping bag

200 ml (¾ cup) cold heavy cream

40 g (⅓ cup) powdered sugar

½ batch Pastry Cream (page 44), chilled

1. In a stand mixer fitted with a whisk attachment, add the heavy cream and powdered sugar and whisk to medium stiff peaks. The mixture should hold its shape on the whisk.

2. Add the pastry cream and use a balloon whisk to loosen it so that it has no lumps and is nice and smooth.

3. Using a spatula, fold in the whipped cream into the pastry cream. Load into a piping bag and use immediately. Do not freeze.

Crème Mousseline
(French Buttercream)

Crème mousseline is a combination of pastry cream and soft butter. It's gorgeous to pipe and is commonly used in building entremets, cake layers, and popular desserts like the Paris-Brest.

Yield: 600 g (21 oz)

Prep Time: 20 minutes

Difficulty: Intermediate

Tools: Stand mixer, piping bag, spatula

½ batch Pastry Cream (page 44), chilled

113 g (½ cup) unsalted butter, at room temperature

65 g (2¼ oz) praline paste, chocolate spread, jam, or other addition of your choice

Chef Tips

Using room-temperature butter is key. If the butter is cold, it will create lumps.

1. In a stand mixer fitted with a whisk or in a large mixing bowl, add the cold pastry cream. Whisk until it is smooth and has no lumps.

2. Add the butter, about 15 g (1 tablespoon) at a time, to the pastry cream as you mix on medium speed. You will see the pastry cream begin to thicken. It should be very smooth. If you notice some lumps from the butter, increase the speed to medium-high.

3. Once you have added half the butter, stop the mixer and scrape down the sides of the bowl. Turn the mixer back up to medium speed and add the rest of the butter, 15 g (1 tablespoon) at a time.

4. Add the praline paste or flavoring of your choice and mix for a few minutes just to combine. Load into a piping bag and get ready to make any cake luxuriously delicious.

Buttercream 101

Buttercream can be tricky to master. Start with the American buttercream if you're a beginner, as it's the easiest one to master. The trick for all of these is that, contrary to the name, we don't want them to taste like butter. They should be sweet, decadent, and creamy. The butter is there for texture more than for flavor. A good-quality, European-style butter with a higher fat content is recommended for buttercream recipes and most baking recipes. See page 48 for more tips on making buttercream.

American Buttercream

Yield: 455 g (16 oz); frosts and fills one 9-inch (23-cm) cake or 24 cupcakes

Prep Time: 20 minutes

Difficulty: Intermediate

Tools: Stand mixer, rubber spatula

---

170 g (¾ cup) unsalted butter, at room temperature

360 g (3 cups) powdered sugar

8 g (2 teaspoons) vanilla bean paste or 2 vanilla beans, split and scraped

40 ml (3 tablespoons) whole milk, plus more as needed, at room temperature

1. In the bowl of a stand mixer fitted with a paddle attachment, add the soft butter, half the powdered sugar, vanilla paste or seeds, and half the milk. Mix together for 10 minutes on high speed. Scrape down the sides of the bowl with a rubber spatula and mix for 5 minutes longer. If starting with cold butter, double the whipping time.

2. Add the rest of the sugar and milk and mix for 5–10 minutes longer. The buttercream should be doubled in size, super creamy, and nice and light. If it still looks a little yellow, mix it for 5 minutes longer. If it is a little too thick, add 2 more teaspoons of milk and mix for 5 more minutes.

3. You can store buttercream in the refrigerator for up to 1 week or freeze it for up to 1 month. When you are ready to use frozen buttercream, move it to the refrigerator the day before and then whip it in the stand mixer. If the buttercream looks "broken" or "split," add 24–36 g (3–4 tablespoons) of powdered sugar as you whip it again to bring it back together. Also make sure the mixture is at room temperature when mixing. If using cold buttercream, it will take twice as long to come back together into a smooth mixture.

Swiss Meringue Buttercream

Prep Time: 20 minutes

Difficulty: Intermediate

Tools: Stand mixer, candy thermometer

210 g (7) egg whites, at room temperature

440 g (2¼ cups) granulated sugar

9 g (2 teaspoons) vanilla bean paste

291 g (1 cup + 2 tablespoons) unsalted butter, at room temperature

1. Wash and dry the stand mixer bowl to make sure there is no grease residue on it. Add the egg whites and sugar. Set the bowl over a bain-marie (double boiler) over low heat. Whisk constantly as you heat up the egg whites. There are two goals here: the first is the egg white mixture needs to reach 160°F (71°C), and the second is we want to make sure the sugar is completely dissolved in the bowl. If you take a small amount of egg mixture between your fingers, you should not feel sugar granules.

2. Place the bowl back on the stand mixer and whisk until stiff peaks form. The meringue will become thick and shiny. Touch the side of the bowl as a test before adding the butter. The bowl should be completely cool to the touch.

3. Switch to the paddle attachment and add the butter, 30 g (2 tablespoons) at a time, to the meringue. Mix on medium speed until completely smooth, thickened, and combined. Use right away.

French Pâte à Bomb Buttercream

Yield: 650 g (23 oz); frosts and fills one 8-inch (20-cm) cake

Prep Time: 20 minutes

Difficulty: Intermediate

Tools: Stand mixer, rubber spatula, candy thermometer, piping bag

200 g (1 cup) granulated sugar

60 ml (¼ cup) water

100 g (2) eggs, at room temperature

291 g (1 cup + 2 tablespoons) unsalted butter, at room temperature

Chef Tips

To flavor pâte à bomb, add vanilla paste, extract, or essence; cocoa powder; or melted chocolate (cooled) to the butter first. Make sure the texture is smooth and then add this to the egg mixture.

1. In a small saucepan, add the sugar and water. Run a spatula through it to make sure the sugar is completely coated in the water and won't stick to the bottom of the pan. As you cook the sugar syrup over medium heat to 250°F (120°C), set up the stand mixer or hand mixer with the eggs. Start whisking them slowly simultaneously.

2. Once the sugar syrup is ready, stream it right away into the eggs as you whisk them on medium speed. Once you have in all of the sugar, increase the mixer to high speed. Whisk for 10 minutes until the eggs have doubled in size and the bowl is cool to the touch.

3. Add the butter about 30 g (2 tablespoons) at a time. Once you have added all the butter, the mixture will thicken significantly. Whisk for 2–3 minutes longer to make sure everything is nice and combined.

4. The pâte à bomb is now ready to use. You can store it in a piping bag in the refrigerator for up to 4 days. You can also freeze it for up to 2 weeks.

Almond Cream

Almond cream is a staple recipe that is used in many French desserts, including almond croissants, bostock, and almandine tarts. You can bake it into a pie crust with berries. It is a versatile cream that will enhance the flavor and texture of any dessert. Traditional almond cream, contrary to almond paste, uses eggs, so it needs to be baked. You can store the cream in a piping bag in the refrigerator and pipe it onto croissants or bread for breakfast and then bake for 20 minutes, or until light golden brown.

Yield: 450 g (16 oz)
Prep Time: 15 minutes
Bake Time: 15–20 minutes
Difficulty: Easy
Tools: Rubber spatula, piping bag

113 g (½ cup) unsalted butter, at room temperature

100 g (1 cup) powdered sugar

4 g (1 teaspoon) vanilla bean paste

2 g (½ teaspoon) almond extract

100 g (2) eggs, at room temperature

100 g (1 cup) almond flour

20 ml (1 tablespoon) dark rum (optional)

1. In a mixing bowl, add the butter and powdered sugar. Mix with a rubber spatula until a smooth paste forms. Add the vanilla paste and almond extract. Mix with the spatula until smooth and well combined, about 1 minute.

2. Add the eggs one at a time, mixing in between each addition for a smooth consistency. Add the almond flour and mix until combined. Add the rum, if using, and mix together.

3. The almond cream is now ready for anything you'd like to do with it. Pipe it onto brioche bread, croissants, or tarts and bake at 350°F (175°C) for 15–20 minutes until light golden brown on top.

4. Store in a piping bag or an airtight container in the refrigerator for up to 1 week.

Variations
Add 25 g (1 oz) of cocoa powder for a chocolaty version.

Almond Paste

Yield: 180 g (6½ oz)
Prep Time: 15 minutes
Difficulty: Easy
Tools: Rubber spatula or balloon whisk

100 g (1 cup) almond flour

50 g (½ cup) powdered sugar

2 g (½ teaspoon) almond extract

30 g (1) egg white, at room temperature

1. In a mixing bowl and using a rubber spatula, combine the almond flour, powdered sugar, and almond extract. Mix until smooth.

2. Add the egg white and mix until a thick paste forms. Use to fill puff pastry squares or already baked goods. Serve as is or bake at 350°F (175°C) until light golden brown, about 15 minutes.

3. Wrap in plastic wrap and store in the refrigerator for up to 1 week.

Frangipane

Many staple recipes in French baking are like building blocks. If you learn one recipe, chances are it will be used in a different preparation to create another mousse or cream. For example, here we are combining pastry cream with almond cream to make frangipane, which is most commonly found in the galette des rois (French kings cake).

Yield: 600 g (21 oz)
Prep Time: 20 minutes
Difficulty: Intermediate
Tools: Rubber spatula

½ batch Pastry Cream (page 44), chilled
½ batch Almond Cream (page 49)

1. Place the pastry cream in a mixing bowl and mix with a rubber spatula to loosen it because it has a stiff consistency coming out of the refrigerator.

2. Add the almond cream and fold the two creams together with a rubber spatula. They will form a smooth, thick cream that can be piped into tart shells, puff pastry, pâte à choux, croissants, and so many other desserts. Bake at 350°F (175°C) for 15–20 minutes, until light golden brown and slightly firm to the touch. Allow to cool before cutting and serving.

Marzipan

Marzipan, though often confused with almond paste, contains much more powdered sugar to make it white and pliable. Many countries still argue over where this delicacy was first created. It has a similar name of *messapian* in various languages.

Yield: 200 g (7 oz)
Prep Time: 15 minutes
Difficulty: Easy
Tools: Food processor

120 g (1¼ cups) blanched almond flour

160 g (1½ cups) powdered sugar

30 g (1) egg white, at room temperature

2 g (½ teaspoon) almond extract

1. In a small food processor, add the almond flour and powdered sugar. Pulse for about 3 minutes to get the mixture nice and smooth. It should be a powdery consistency with no lumps.

2. Add half of the egg white and the almond extract. Pulse to combine. It should come together and just be slightly sticky, depending on how humid or dry the almond flour is. The weather can also impact how much egg white you need to add. You want to add just enough to form the marzipan and be able to mold it. If you add too much egg white, the mixture will be very sticky and more of a paste than a sliceable consistency.

3. Place the marzipan on a piece of plastic wrap and roll into a log. Keep airtight in the plastic wrap in the refrigerator for up to 2 weeks. Use for cake decorations, or slice up and dip into chocolate and enjoy as is.

Variations
You can use other nut flours, such as pistachio or hazelnut.

Homemade Hazelnut Chocolate Spread

Is there anything more nostalgic than the perfect homemade chocolate spread on a warm piece of brioche bread? This classic recipe is made with hazelnuts, but you can also try it with cashews or almonds. This chocolate spread combines my liquid gold praline paste, chocolate, sugar, and a little oil to make it nice and spreadable. Get ready to spread this on absolutely everything you make. Think of it as your favorite store-bought spread, but better.

Yield: 400 g (about 1½ cups)

Prep Time: 20 minutes

Difficulty: Intermediate

Tools: Food processor, rubber spatula

---

150 g (¾ cup) granulated sugar

250 g (2 cups) all-purpose flour

7 g (1½ teaspoons) baking powder

100 g (2) eggs, at room temperature

100 g (⅔ cup) whole toasted hazelnuts (no skin)

80 g (¾ cup) powdered sugar

200 g (1 cup) Hazelnut Praline Paste (page 53)

120 g (¾ cup) milk chocolate chips

20 ml (1½ tablespoons) grapeseed oil or neutral oil

20 g (2 tablespoons + 2 teaspoons) unsweetened cocoa powder

100 g (3½ oz) toasted almonds

1. In a food processor, add the hazelnuts and pulse for several minutes until you get a powdery texture. Add the powdered sugar and pulse for several minutes, until thickened and clumpy.

2. Add the praline paste and mix for 2–3 more minutes until smooth.

3. In a small microwave-safe bowl, add the chocolate chips and oil and melt in 20-second increments, stirring in between each interval. Once fully melted, but still warm and smooth, add the chocolate mixture to the food processor. Pulse for 2 minutes until combined.

4. Add the cocoa powder. Scrape down the sides of the food processor and mix for 2 minutes longer, until everything its completely smooth.

5. Pour into a jar with a lid and store at room temperature for up to 1 week.

Variation

Try substituting the milk chocolate for a 60 percent or 70 percent dark chocolate for a less sweet, but equally delicious spread.

Hazelnut Praline Paste

This is toasted and caramelized creamy heaven, also known as liquid gold that you will want to spread and use in everything you make. There are a few methods for making this addictive paste, but the result is the same golden goodness.

Yield: 300 g (10¾ oz)

Prep Time: 20 minutes

Cook Time: 10 minutes

Difficulty: Easy

Tools: Food processor, rubber spatula

300 g (10¾ oz) whole raw hazelnuts (no skin)

200 g (1 cup) granulated sugar

100 ml (6 tablespoons) water

30 ml (2 tablespoons) grapeseed oil or neutral oil

1. Preheat the oven to 300°F (150°C). Line a baking sheet with a silicone mat or parchment paper.

2. Spread the hazelnuts on the prepared baking sheet and toast them in the oven for 5 minutes to get them lightly golden brown and release those nutty aromas. Let cool.

3. In a 3- or 4-qt (2.7- or 3.6-L) saucepan, add the sugar and water. Make sure the saucepan is very clean and there is no sugar on the sides. The sugar should be perfectly coated in water. Cook over medium heat until the mixture starts to bubble. DO NOT STIR. Let cook for 5–7 minutes, until it is amber in color. Once it is nice and golden brown, pour it over the warm toasted hazelnuts. Let the caramel harden and cool completely.

4. Break the caramel and nuts into 2- or 3-inch (5- or 7.5-cm) pieces and place them in a food processor. Pulse for 5 minutes. Stop every 2 minutes and scrape down the sides of the processor. The mixture will start to form a thick paste. Drizzle in the oil 15 ml (1 tablespoon) at a time as you continue to pulse the hazelnut paste.

5. Once the mixture is a thick pourable consistency, pour it into a jar and store in the refrigerator for up to 1 month. Add to pastry cream, crepes, warm bread, buttercreams, whipped creams, or ice cream base. It works with just about everything.

Chocolate Ganache 101

Rumor has it that ganache got its name from the "idiot" who poured hot heavy cream on the chocolate when he wasn't supposed to. (*Ganache* means "idiot" in French.) There's no proof of this, but it makes for a great anecdote. But what is chocolate ganache? It is a fancy way of describing the emulsification process between chocolate and heavy cream. Ganache is all about the ratio between the chocolate and the liquid (cream), and it can be used in many different ratios for cakes, mousses, creams, and chocolates. The process to make each one is the same.

Yield: 240 or 360 g (8⅓ or 13 oz)
Prep Time: 5 minutes
Cook Time: 5 minutes
Difficulty: Easy
Tools: Balloon whisk, stand mixer

Ganache 1:1 Ratio

120 g (¾ cup) dark chocolate chips

120 g (½ cup) heavy cream

Ganache 2:1 Ratio

240 g (1½ cups) dark chocolate chips

120 g (½ cup) heavy cream

Ganache 1:2 Ratio

120 g (¾ cup) dark chocolate chips

240 g (1 cup) heavy cream

1. Place the chocolate chips in a heat-proof bowl.

2. Pour the cream into a 2-qt (1.8-L) saucepan. Bring it to a boil over high heat, and then pour it over the dark chocolate chips. Let stand for 20 seconds, and then whisk together until smooth and combined. The mixture will go from looking like chocolate milk to a thick smooth and shiny chocolate spread.

3. For a whipped ganache, refrigerate the ganache overnight so it gets nice and cold. The next day, pour the ganache into a stand mixer or use a hand mixer to whip until stiff peaks form. This whips very similarly to a thick, chocolaty whipped cream.

Chef Tips

- The 1:1 ratio makes a silky smooth ganache that is spreadable and great for creating those drip effects on the sides of a cake.
- The 2:1 ratio makes a thicker ganache perfect for truffles or for piping onto cakes or cookies.
- The 1:2 ratio makes a thick chocolate whipped cream that you can use between cake layers. It's also great with a plate of fresh berries.
- If you want to use white or milk chocolate, you will need to use more chocolate because they have less cacao mass.

Pretty Buttery Crepes

This recipe is dear to my heart. When I was little, early mornings in Paris were spent baking and eating crepes that my grandmother made. The sweet smell of vanilla, sugar, and butter engulfed the entire house. You have to get the batter just right to make them very thin and soft. Resting the batter allows the gluten to relax and the flavors to blend together. Mom would also make these Saturday mornings, accompanied by a full hour of cartoon time. These have a very small amount of sugar, which you can omit if you want to make savory crepes.

Yield: Fifteen 9-inch (23-cm) crepes

Prep Time: 10 minutes

Rest Time: 6 hours, or overnight

Cook Time: 3–4 minutes each

Difficulty: Easy

Tools: Crepe pan, ladle, balloon whisk

160 g (1¼ cups) all-purpose flour

50 g (¼ cup) granulated sugar

470 ml (2 cups) whole milk, at room temperature

200 g (4) eggs, at room temperature

8 g (2 teaspoons) vanilla bean paste

50 g (4 tablespoons) unsalted butter, melted

20 ml (1 tablespoon) dark rum or Cointreau (optional)

40 ml (2 tablespoons) grapeseed oil or neutral oil

Unsalted butter, at room temperature, for cooking

Chef Tips

Make sure to use milk at room temperature. If you add melted butter to cold milk, the butter will firm up and create lumps.

1. In a mixing bowl with a balloon whisk, combine the flour and sugar. Mix together for 1 minute to get rid of any lumps.

2. In a separate mixing bowl, add the milk, eggs, vanilla, melted butter, rum (if using), and grapeseed oil. Whisk until smooth, 2 minutes. Make sure all the ingredients are at room temperature or the butter will solidify in the cold milk, creating lumps.

3. Stream the milk mixture into the flour mixture as you whisk the batter together. Whisk until completely smooth with no lumps. If you have a few stubborn lumps, run the batter through a strainer.

4. Place the batter in the refrigerator overnight, or for at least 6 hours.

5. Heat a crepe pan over medium heat and prepare a small bowl of soft butter to keep brushing on the pan in between each crepe. The first 2–3 crepes may not be perfect as you learn the right thickness and cooking time. Brush a small amount of butter on the pan. Using a ladle, add a small amount of batter, then twist and angle the pan downward in a clockwise motion to coat it evenly. Cook over medium heat for 2 minutes until the edges get light golden brown and detach from the pan. Then flip to the other side. Slide the spatula underneath to the middle of the crepe to flip it easily. Cook for 1 more minute, until the crepe is golden on both sides. Stack the crepes on top of each other to keep them warm.

6. You can make a bunch of crepes in advance and warm them for a few seconds in the microwave or in a pan to keep the perfect texture. They will keep baked and covered for up to 4 days in the refrigerator. You can keep the uncooked batter covered in the refrigerator for up to 3 days and bake crepes fresh every morning.

Variations

To serve these crepes with something savory like ham, cheese, or eggs, simply remove the sugar from the recipe and add a pinch of salt. Do not add pepper, because the pepper will burn in the batter.

Fluffy Pancakes

Pancakes are simple, but fluffy pancakes are made with a special trick that makes them even more irresistible. The melted butter and buttermilk are the secret ingredients in this recipe. The acidity in the buttermilk activates the baking soda, making the pancakes extra light and airy. If you add in the French meringue, it will create delicious soufflé-like pancakes, a Japanese technique that makes pancakes fluffier and thicker than usual.

Yield: 600 g (21 oz), 8–10 pancakes

Prep Time: 10 minutes

Rest Time: 6 hours (if making without the meringue)

Cook Time: 5 minutes each

Difficulty: Easy

Tools: Ladle, balloon whisk, 6-inch (15-cm) cookie cutter (for the soufflé pancakes)

180 g (1½ cups) all-purpose flour

6 g (1 teaspoon) baking soda

30 g (2 tablespoons) granulated sugar

100 g (2) eggs, at room temperature

235 ml (1 cup) buttermilk, at room temperature

60 g (¼ cup) unsalted butter, melted

8 g (2 teaspoons) vanilla bean paste

French Meringue (optional)

30 g (1) egg white, at room temperature

30 g (2 tablespoons) granulated sugar

Unsalted butter, at room temperature, for cooking

1. In a mixing bowl, add the flour, baking soda, and sugar. Use a balloon whisk to mix for 1 minute to get rid of any lumps.

2. In a separate mixing bowl, add the eggs, buttermilk, melted butter, and vanilla. Whisk until smooth, about 2 minutes. Make sure your ingredients are at room temperature for a smooth batter. Stream this mixture into the flour mixture as you whisk the batter. Whisk until completely smooth; there should be no lumps at all. If you have a few stubborn lumps, run the batter through a strainer.

3. If you want even fluffier pancakes, make the French meringue: In a small bowl, whip the egg white with the sugar and gently fold into the pancake batter so as not to deflate the egg white. Cook right away. Do not store for later use. Add 2–3 minutes to the cooking time for each pancake.

4. If making the version without the added meringue, let the batter rest in the refrigerator overnight, or for at least 6 hours for the best results.

5. Place a nonstick pan over medium heat and prepare a bowl of soft butter to keep brushing on the pan in between each pancake. For the regular pancake, place a small amount of batter evenly on the pan and cook for 2 minutes, then flip to the other side with a spatula and cook for an additional 2–3 minutes. For the soufflé pancakes, brush a 6-inch (15-cm) round cookie cutter with butter. Place it on the nonstick pan and pour the batter into the ring. This will create a nice tall thick shape. Let cook for 3 minutes, then flip over using a spatula, keeping the ring around the batter. Cook for 3 minutes until golden brown on the other side. Remove the ring, cover the pan with a lid, and cook for 2 minutes more. You can add 30 ml (2 tablespoons) of water to the pan to create some steam when covered.

6. Store the plain batter without the whipped egg white in an airtight jar for up to 2 days in the refrigerator.

Caramel 101

There are two main techniques used to make caramel. One is wet caramel and the other is dry caramel; the first simply includes a small amount of water, and the other does not. Caramel can be tricky, but it is an important base recipe to master because you can use it in hundreds of ways in baking. I recommend starting with the wet caramel, as I find it easier.

Yield: 250 g (about 1 cup)
Prep Time: 5 minutes
Cook Time: 8–10 minutes
Difficulty: Intermediate

250 g (1¼ cups) granulated sugar
100 ml (¼ cup) water

Chef Tips

- Use fresh sugar—older sugar will have more humidity in it that can cause it to mass or crystalize when it's cooking.
- Use a clean saucepan, and use a pastry brush to brush down the sides of the pan with tiny amount of water as the sugar begins to cook.
- Adding a small amount of inverted sugar, such as glucose or honey, can stop your caramel from crystalizing.
- DO NOT STIR your caramel once the sugar begins to boil.
- Have the pan that you will pour your caramel into prepared in advance, as caramel will go from perfectly amber to burned very quickly. You can also prepare an ice bath to plunge the pan into to stop the cooking process.
- If you happen to overcook your caramel or it sticks to the pot, simply pour water into the pan and bring to a boil to remove all the caramel.

Wet Caramel

1. In a 3- or 4-qt (2.7- or 3.6-l) saucepan, add the sugar and water. Run a rubber spatula along the bottom of the pan to make sure all of the sugar is coated in the water. Cook over medium-high heat for 5 minutes, as the mixture starts to boil; DO NOT stir it at all. Cook until the color goes from lightly golden to dark amber. This should take 8–10 minutes total.

2. As the sugar begins to caramelize, keep an eye on it at all times, as it can darken and burn quickly. Use the caramel as soon as it's ready before it sets.

Dry Caramel

1. Pour half of the sugar into the saucepan. Cook over medium-high heat, and as the sugar starts to caramelize, move it around gently with a wooden spoon or rubber spatula. Keep adding the sugar little by little as it continues to melt and caramelize, moving it around gently to break up any sugar pieces. This method takes a few extra minutes the first time. If the temperature is too high it will burn the sugar. Once cooked, use the caramel right away before it sets.

Thick Salted Butter Caramel Sauce

The emblematic salted butter caramel owes its origin to Brittany. They were among the first perfect the salted butter and used this dessert to show it off. However something this delicious doesn't stay secret for long. In 1906 a in the small town of Bordeaux was born one of the most famous confiseries (sweets shop) famous for these sweet creamy buttery caramels. Simple ingredients create this delicious sauce you will want to put on absolutely everything.

Yield: 400 g (2 cups)

Prep Time: 20 minutes

Difficulty: Easy

Tools: Rubber spatula, balloon whisk

---

140 g (¾ cup) granulated sugar

235 ml (1¼ cups) heavy cream

100 g (1/2 cup) unsalted butter, at room temperature

2 g (1 pinch) flaky sea salt

1. In a 3- or 4-qt (2.7- or 3.6-l) saucepan, add the sugar and 100 ml (5 tablespoons) water to coat the sugar. Run a rubber spatula along the bottom of the pan to make sure all of the sugar is coated by the water. Cook on medium-high heat for 5 minutes; as the mixture starts to boil DO NOT stir it at all. Cook until the color goes from lightly golden to dark amber color. It should take 8 to 10 minutes total.

2. As the sugar begins to caramelize, keep your eye on it all times; it can darken and burn very quickly.

3. When your caramel is ready, lower the heat to medium, then slowly pour the heavy cream into the mixture in increments, whisking constantly. Be careful, as the sauce will bubble up and then back down each time. Once you have added all your heavy cream, whisk gently to make sure the mix is well combined.

4. Next, add in your softened butter about 15 g (1 tablespoon) at a time. Whisk in between each addition to keep the caramel smooth. Lastly, add your sea salt and whisk gently to combine well.

5. Pour into a glass jar and let cool to room temperature. Store in the refrigerator for up to 1 week and spread on everything.

Homemade Ladyfingers
(Biscuits a la Cuillere)

As the story goes, these little "biscuits" were invented in the early nineteenth century by a French pastry chef named Marie-Antoine (known as "Antonin") Carême. They have been amended over the years and are extremely popular to use as layers in desserts such as tiramisu and the classic charlotte. These are beautiful lined up in a row to wrap the entire cake along the outside or can be stacked as individual cake layers on the inside.

Yield: 24 ladyfingers or 12 ladyfingers + 2 disks

Prep Time: 20 minutes

Bake Time: 15 minutes

Difficulty: Intermediate

Tools: Stand mixer, piping bag, silicone mat, sifter, spatula

---

250 g (5) eggs, at room temperature, separated

140 g (⅔ cup) granulated sugar, divided

120 g (1 cup) all-purpose flour

50 g (½ cup) powdered sugar, for dusting

Chef Tips

- *The only leavening in these is mechanical, which comes from whipping the egg whites and whipping the egg yolks to make them nice and fluffy. Take your time whipping the egg whites to stiff peaks and the yolks to the ribbon stage (page 22).*
- *Make sure you do not get any egg yolks in the whites, or they will not whip to stiff peaks.*

1. Preheat the oven to 300°F (150°C). Line two baking sheets with silicone mats or parchment paper.

2. Place the egg whites in a stand mixer fitted with a whisk attachment or a mixing bowl. Add half of the granulated sugar and whisk on medium speed until stiff peaks form, about 10 minutes. The egg whites will hold their shape on the whisk, be smooth and shiny, and pull away from the sides of the bowl.

3. In a separate bowl, while you whip the egg whites, whip the egg yolks with the remaining granulated sugar. The mixture should double in volume and be pale in color (blanchir).

4. Gently fold the egg yolk mixture into the egg white mixture by hand using a rubber spatula. Alternate some yolk mixture and some flour to get everything incorporated perfectly. Make sure to fold gently and reach the bottom and sides of the bowl. Take your time.

5. Load the mixture into a piping bag (no need for a piping tip) and decide what you would like to do. You can make 24 ladyfingers or 12 ladyfingers plus 2 disks.

6. To pipe ladyfingers: Pipe into 2 x 1-inch (5 x 2.5-cm) sticks. You can pipe them next to each other so they all stick together and can be used to cover the outside of a cake. This is called a "cartouche." You can also pipe them individually spaced 2–3 inches apart, so that you can use them in preparations like tiramisu.

7. To pipe disks: Pipe two 9-inch (23-cm) round disks in a spiral motion. These can also be used as cake layers in various recipes.

8. Using the sifter, dust the top with powdered sugar before placing them in the oven. Bake until lightly golden brown, 12–15 minutes. Do not attempt to remove them from the mat until they cool completely. Store in an airtight container for up to 3 days, or use right away to build your next cake.

Poaching Liquid for Stone Fruits

This poaching liquid is often used to precook pears, apples, peaches, and larger stone fruits before using them in a dessert. I love to add some white wine in this recipe, especially when cooking pears, for extra depth of flavor. You can replace it with red wine to infuse that gorgeous color into the fruits. Try to always use whole vanilla beans for maximum flavor, as extracts will not give you the same results.

Yield: 1 l (4 cups)
Prep Time: 20 minutes
Difficulty: Easy
Tools: Rubber spatula, jars with lids

800 ml (3⅓ cups) water
200 ml (¾ cup) white wine
250 g (1¼ cups) granulated sugar
3 vanilla beans

Chef Tips

- Respect the amount of liquid in the recipe. If you don't want to use wine, replace that weight with water or a pure unsweetened fruit juice. I prefer using alcohol-free wine for the acidity it brings to counterbalance the sweetness. It's also a neutral flavor that works with many different fruits.

- To scrape a vanilla bean, lay the bean on a cutting board and flatten it gently with the back of a paring knife, holding the curved tip between your fingers to keep it in place. Cut through the whole bean lengthwise and use the back of the knife to scrape out the seeds. Add both the beans and the seeds to your liquid.

1. In a 3- or 4-qt (2.7- or 3.6-l) saucepan, combine the water, wine, and sugar. Split and scrape the vanilla beans and add both the seeds and the bean pods to the pan. Bring to a boil over high heat, mix with a spatula to make sure nothing sticks to the bottom, and then reduce to a simmer. Let simmer for several minutes so the flavors infuse together.

2. When ready to poach the fruit, simply reheat the poaching liquid and drop in the cored fruit. Cook the fruit just until tender. When you insert a knife, they should still have a little resistance and be slightly firm. Use the fruit right away in desserts.

3. Store the liquid in airtight jars in the refrigerator for up to 2 weeks. Strain the liquid each time you are done using it and you can reuse it until it runs out.

Simple Syrup

Simple syrup is great to have on hand—it can be used to soak cake layers or in many different baking preparations. It is usually equal parts water and sugar. What is fun is infusing it with different citrus zests, vanilla, or cinnamon sticks for added flavor.

Yield: 400 ml (2 cups)

Prep Time: 20 minutes

Cook Time: 5–10 minutes

Difficulty: Easy

Tools: Saucepan, rubber spatula, jars with lids

200 ml (¾ cup) water

200 g (1 cup) granulated sugar

Zest of 1 lemon

Zest of 1 orange

1. In a 3- or 4-qt (2.7- or 3.6-l) saucepan, add the water, sugar, and citrus zests. Bring to a boil over medium heat, stirring occasionally with a rubber spatula to dissolve the sugar.

2. Reduce the heat and simmer for 5 minutes. Once the sugar is completely dissolved, pour the liquid into a glass jar, leaving the zests, and store in the refrigerator for future use for up to 3 weeks.

Variations

If infusing cinnamon for spiced syrup, use cinnamon sticks and star anise for the best depth of flavor. You can leave them in the jar in the refrigerator. Taste often, as the flavor will continue to develop when using a strong spice like cinnamon.

Small Bites

Les Bouchées

The definition of a great dessert does not need to be something complex or difficult to put together. It is about finding the perfect balance of textures, tastes, and consistency to create the perfect bite. The French love petits fours and bite-size delicacies. This chapter has a wonderful selection of the perfect bite-size goodies for all kinds of occasions. Elegance in every bite.

Granny's Famous Biscotti

This is one of the first recipes I ever wrote, and I dedicate it to my granny. She was a very dedicated taste-tester, as I would make these over and over to reach that perfect crunch and crispy texture, without them being overly hard to bite. I would bring them back from my Parisian bakery every weekend for granny to enjoy with her morning coffee. These will become a favorite in the household, guaranteed.

Yield: 70–80 small biscotti

Prep Time: 15 minutes

Rest Time: 30–40 minutes

Bake Time: 50 minutes

Difficulty: Easy

Tools: Cutting board, chef's knife, spatula

150 g (¾ cup) granulated sugar

250 g (2 cups) all-purpose flour

7 g (1½ teaspoons) baking powder

100 g (2) eggs, at room temperature

100 g (3½ oz) toasted almonds

1. In a large mixing bowl, combine the sugar, flour, and baking powder. Mix well to combine.

2. Add the eggs and mix just enough so everything is combined. The dough will be sticky and a little shaggy. Do not overmix or overwork the dough. Add the toasted almonds and mix again.

3. Using a baking scale, divide the dough into six balls of 100 g (3½ oz) each.

4. Line a baking sheet with a silicone mat or parchment paper and set aside. Sprinkle a little flour onto the work surface to keep the dough from sticking. Roll each ball into a log and place on the prepared baking sheet. Make sure you carefully space out the logs on the sheet, as each one will double in size when they bake, and you don't want them to stick to each other. Allow the logs to rest for 30–40 minutes, depending on the humidity, until no longer sticky to the touch.

5. Preheat the oven to 350°F (175°C).

6. Transfer the baking sheet to the oven and bake for 40 minutes, until the logs have doubled in size and are golden brown.

7. Remove the baking sheet from the oven, transfer one log at a time to the cutting board, and work quickly to slice the biscotti at an angle from each log. Each log should yield 12–14 biscotti, depending on the angle you're cutting.

8. Lay all of the biscotti flat on the baking mat and place back in the oven for 5 minutes, then remove, flip the biscotti onto the other cut side, and bake for 5 minutes longer. This is a very important step to finish drying out the biscotti correctly.

9. Remove the baking sheet from the oven. Slide the silicone mat off of the sheet onto the counter. This will stop the baking process to keep the biscotti from getting too hard or overbaked.

10. Once cooled, store in an airtight container for up to 6 weeks.

Variations

You can make these biscotti into any flavor you want. When creating your own version, you can replace the almonds with 100 g (3½ oz) of whatever you are adding to keep the ratios of the recipe exact. You can use dried cranberries, mini chocolate chips, toasted hazelnuts, or coconut. I used to make a delicious pistachio version in my Parisian bakery: I would add 20 g (¾ oz) of dried rose petals and 80 g (2¾ oz) of pistachios.

Old-Fashioned Macarons
(Macarons a l'ancienne)

Maison Adam in Saint-Jean-de-Luz in France has been making these delicate cookies for more than 360 years, and they have quite the world reputation. They were first introduced as a special dessert for the wedding of Louis XIV and quickly adopted soon after for all festivities and celebratory occasions. These are known as old-fashioned French macarons. Contrary to the classic French sandwich cookie, these macarons come together very easily and the almond flour and powdered sugar produce a unique, chewy meringue texture from the almond flour and powdered sugar with none of the fuss.

Yield: 40–50 cookies

Prep Time: 10 minutes

Bake Time: 15–20 minutes (depending on size)

Difficulty: Easy

Tools: Silicone mat, stand mixer, rubber spatula, piping bag, sifter

---

250 g (2⅔ cups) almond flour

200 g (1¾ cups) powdered sugar, plus more for dusting

120 g (4) egg whites, at room temperature

4 g (1 teaspoon) vanilla bean paste

2 g (½ teaspoon) almond extract

Chef Tips

Use egg whites at room temperature for a chewier cookie. Cold egg whites are much harder to incorporate into the batter to get the right consistency. To get your eggs quickly to room temperature, add them to bowl of hot water for 10 minutes. Doing this will also make it much easier to separate the whites from the yolks.

1. Preheat the oven to 325°F (160°C). Line two baking sheets with parchment paper or silicone mats.

2. In the bowl of a stand mixer fitted with a paddle attachment, or by hand with a spatula, add the almond flour and powdered sugar and mix for 1 minute.

3. In a separate bowl, add the eggs whites, vanilla, and almond extract and mix together. Stream into the dry ingredients as you mix on medium speed. The batter should be smooth and combined. Use a spatula to break up any lumps. Scrape down the sides of the bowl and mix for 1 minute longer. Transfer the batter to a piping bag fitted with a small round tip or pipe without one.

4. Pipe small round cookies, evenly spaced and offset, onto the prepared baking sheets and dust with a little powdered sugar right before baking.

5. Bake for 15–20 minutes, until the entire cookie is golden brown. The bottoms should also be golden brown. Remove from the oven and slide off the hot baking sheet to stop the baking process. Let the macarons cool completely to room temperature before removing them from the paper or silicone mat.

6. Store in an airtight container at room temperature for up to 2 weeks.

Crispy Oatmeal Milk Chocolate Chip Cookies

Do not talk to me about oatmeal raisin cookies, but oatmeal chocolate chip—yes, that is a match made in heaven. The creaminess of the milk chocolate is a wonderful texture contrast with the crunchy oats and cinnamon. These cookies come together in 10 minutes and they are sure to satisfy any sweet craving. You can also use these for delicious ice cream sandwiches in the summer and keep them in the freezer to have on hand.

Yield: 16 large cookies

Prep Time: 10 minutes

Chill Time: 30 minutes

Bake Time: 15–20 minutes

Difficulty: Easy

Tools: Silicone mat, balloon whisk, rubber spatula,

---

170 g (¾ cup) unsalted butter, melted

220 g (1 cup) light brown sugar

125 g (⅔ cup) granulated sugar

50 g (1) egg, at room temperature

20 g (1) egg yolk, at room temperature

30 ml (2 tablespoons) maple syrup

2 g (¾ teaspoon) ground cinnamon

200 g (1⅔ cups) all-purpose flour

120 g (1⅓ cups) rolled oats

8 g (1½ teaspoons) baking soda

220 g (1⅓ cups) milk chocolate chips

1. Line a baking sheet with a silicone mat or parchment paper.

2. In a large bowl, add the melted butter, brown sugar, and granulated sugar and whisk until smooth and combined. Add the egg and mix for 2 minutes longer. Add the yolk and mix for 2 minutes longer. Add the maple syrup and cinnamon and mix to combine.

3. In a separate bowl, add the flour, rolled oats, and baking soda. Mix to combine. Add the dry ingredients to the butter mixture. Mix together to form the dough. Add the chocolate chips and fold once more to combine. Place the dough in the freezer for 30 minutes.

4. When ready to bake, preheat the oven to 350°F (175°C). Form the dough into balls weighing 50 g (scant 2 oz). Roll each one into a perfect ball and place on the prepared baking sheet, scattering them, but not placing them in a row because these will spread when baking.

5. Bake for 15–20 minutes, or until dark golden brown. Slide the silicone mat gently off the baking sheet without disturbing the cookies. Allow them to cool before handling them. They're soft and chewy.

6. Store in an airtight container at room temperature for up to 5 days. Store the unbaked cookie dough in the refrigerator wrapped in plastic wrap and bake all week long for fresh cookies. You can also roll the cookie dough into balls and store the balls in a zip-top bag in the freezer for up to 1 month, and bake them right from frozen. Simply add 5 minutes to the baking time.

Fudgy Brownie Cookies

Are you an edge piece lover from the brownie pan? Then these are for you.
They have all the decadence of the perfect gooey brownie in cookie form, except now
you get the best part in every bite, with that chewy exterior and gooey center.

Yield: 24 cookies of 35 g
(1½ oz) each

Prep Time: 20 minutes

Rest Time: 2–4 hours

Bake Time: 12 minutes

Difficulty: Easy

Tools: Stand mixer, spatula,
silicone mat

125 g (9 tablespoons)
unsalted butter, at room
temperature

220 g (1½ cups) dark chocolate
(at least 60 percent)

100 g (½ cup) granulated sugar

100 g (½ cup) dark brown sugar

100 g (2) eggs, at room
temperature

4 g (1 teaspoon) vanilla bean paste

120 g (1 cup) all-purpose flour

5 g (1 teaspoon) baking powder

22 g (3 tablespoons) cocoa
powder

100 g (¾ cup) milk chocolate chips

2 g (½ teaspoon) flaky sea salt
(optional)

1. In a microwave-safe bowl, add the butter and dark chocolate. Melt in 20-second increments, stirring slowly in between each interval, until completely melted; set aside.

2. In a stand mixer fitted with the whisk attachment or with a hand whisk, add the sugars, eggs, and vanilla. Whisk together on medium speed until the mixture doubles in size. It should be thick and pale in color. This works a lot faster if you are using eggs at room temperature. If you are using cold eggs, it will take 12–15 minutes.

3. Once the egg mixture is ready, reduce the speed to low and slowly stream in the melted chocolate mixture.

4. In a separate bowl, combine the flour, baking powder, cocoa powder, and milk chocolate chips. Add the dry ingredients to the egg mixture all at once. Fold the mixture gently by hand with a rubber spatula or with the paddle attachment on a stand mixer until the dough comes together. Cover with plastic wrap and store in the refrigerator for 2–4 hours.

5. When you are ready to bake, preheat the oven to 375°F (190°C). Line two baking sheets with silicone mats or parchment paper.

6. Using a tablespoon or small ice cream scoop, scoop out amounts of the dough onto the baking scale. Each cookie should weigh 35 g (1½ oz). Roll them into balls to compress the dough for more even baking. Place them on the prepared baking sheet spaced 2 inches apart, with no more than 10 cookies per baking sheet to allow for proper airflow around the cookies in the oven.

7. Flatten the cookies ever so slightly and add a touch of flaky sea salt, if desired. Bake for 12 minutes, until the cookies are soft to the touch but hold their shape. They will not spread. Remove from the oven, slide the baking mat off the baking sheet, and allow to cool to room temperature for about 10 minutes before enjoying them.

8. Store them in an airtight container for up to 1 week. The dough can also be frozen for up to 1 month and baked from frozen; simply added 3–4 minutes to the baking time.

Variations

For a sweeter cookie and slightly less dark chocolate, feel free to swap the dark chocolate chips for milk chocolate chips. This cookie is rich and decadent, so I recommend baking it in the small size given here.

Florentine Bars

It's the beginning of the Renaissance. Anne of Brittany has just married
the king of France, Louis XII. As a gift, she receives the house of Medici in Florence.
She throws a wonderful soiree and decides to surprise her guests with a special treat. She asks
her chef to prepare original culinary delights sure to wow the crowd. Well-versed in Italian
flavors and specialties, the chef combines chocolate, butter, citrus zest, and sliced almonds.
He makes them round and thin and coats the bottom with chocolate. Rumor has it,
this is how florentine cookies were born.

Yield: 14–16 bars

Prep Time: 30 minutes

Rest Time: 2 hours

Bake Time: 30 minutes

Difficulty: Intermediate

Tools: Stand mixer, rubber spatula, silicone mat, candy thermometer, offset spatula, chef's knife

For the Sable Dough

143 g (½ cup + 2 tablespoons) unsalted butter, at room temperature

100 g (½ cup) granulated sugar

4 g (1 teaspoon) vanilla bean paste

2 g (½ teaspoon) almond extract

50 g (1) egg, at room temperature

200 g (1⅔ cups) all-purpose flour

30 g (5 tablespoons) almond flour

30 g (4 tablespoons) cornstarch

For the Almond Caramel Topping

100 g (½ cup) granulated sugar

20 g (1 tablespoon) honey

40 ml (2 tablespoons + 2 teaspoons) water

30 g (2 tablespoons) unsalted butter, at room temperature

60 ml (¼ cup) heavy cream

180 g (2½ cups) sliced untoasted almonds

1. To make the sable dough: In a stand mixer fitted with a paddle attachment, add the butter, sugar, vanilla, and almond extract. Beat on medium speed for 5 minutes, until the mixture is nice and creamy. Scrape down the sides of the bowl and beat for 2 minutes longer. The mix should be pale in color and a little fluffy. Add the egg and mix for 2–3 minutes, until the batter is back to perfectly smooth and fluffy. Work with eggs at room temperature.

2. Add the all-purpose flour, almond flour, and cornstarch. Pulse for a few seconds on medium speed just to combine and form a dough. If you overmix the dough it will get very sticky. Finish mixing the dough by hand in the bowl to get it perfectly combined.

3. Line a baking sheet with a silicone mat and place the dough in the center. Place another mat or parchment paper on top of the dough. Using a rolling pin, flatten the dough to ¼ inch (6 mm) thick and as even as possible into a rectangular shape. DO NOT try to remove the top parchment paper until after cooling the dough or it will rip right off. Place the baking sheet in the freezer for 2 hours to allow the dough to fully harden.

4. When ready to bake, preheat the oven to 350°F (175°C).

5. Remove the baking sheet from the freezer and gently peel off one of the mats or parchment papers. Trim the edges to create a perfect rectangle. Bake for 15 minutes, until the surface and edges are lightly golden brown; the center will stay fairly white.

6. While the sable dough is baking, prepare the caramel: In a small saucepan, add the sugar, honey, and water. The water should wet the sugar and create a wet sand consistency. Make sure the sugar is fully covered in water. Stir to make sure the sugar is not sticking to the bottom. Once the mixture begins to boil, DO NOT STIR. Cook over medium heat until the caramel is a nice, light golden color and reaches 320°F (160°C) on a candy thermometer.

7. Add the butter to the caramel, and whisk until smooth (this is called deglazing). Add the heavy cream in two increments and whisk until smooth. Lastly, add the almonds and mix until completely coated.

8. Pour this mixture right away on top of the baked sable crust and use an offset spatula to spread it evenly so it covers the whole surface. Return the pan to the oven and bake for 15–20 minutes, until golden.

9. Remove from the oven and let sit for just a few minutes. You want to cut these bars while they are still warm because it will be much easier to do while the caramel is soft. Using a chef's knife, cut once horizontally across the middle and then slice vertically to get about fourteen to sixteen bars. Let cool completely.

10. Store in an airtight container for up to 1 week.

11. You can prepare the sable dough in advance and even keep it already rolled out in the freezer until ready to use. If baking right from frozen, add a few minutes to the baking time.

Monsieur Hazelnut Financier

The financier is an iconic bite-size French pastry found in almost all patisseries. This little delicate pastry was well liked by French businessmen who worked in finance in the early 1900s, and that's where it gets its name. It's a very delicate almond pastry that leaves no crumbs behind in case you want to sneak one at the office.

Yield: 12 financiers

Prep Time: 10 minutes

Bake Time: 8 minutes or 12 minutes (depending on size)

Difficulty: Intermediate

Tools: Rubber spatula, financier pan or pans, piping bag, pastry brush

---

100 g (1 cup) almond flour

80 g (⅔ cup) all-purpose flour

50 g (½ cup) hazelnut flour

150 g (1⅓ cups) powdered sugar

227 g (1 cup) unsalted butter, plus more for the pan

150 g (5) egg whites

80 g (¼ cup) Hazelnut Praline Paste (page 53)

100 g (⅔ cup) chopped hazelnuts, for topping

1. In a stand mixer fitted with a paddle attachment or in a mixing bowl by hand, add the almond flour, all-purpose flour, hazelnut flour, and powdered sugar and mix to combine.

2. In a small saucepan, add the butter and simmer over low heat until melted. Carefully reduce to heat to brown the butter slowly to a nice amber color. DO NOT BURN. Let cool to room temperature.

3. Stream the egg whites into the flour mixture one at a time. It is crucial that there are no lumps, so be sure to to mix the batter continuously as you are adding the egg whites. Scrape down the sides of the bowl and mix for another minute, just until everything is nice and smooth.

4. Add the room-temperature brown butter, streaming it slowly into the batter as you mix on low speed. Lastly, add in the praline paste and mix 1 more minute, until smooth and incorporated. Pour the batter into a piping bag (no tip needed) and set aside.

5. Preheat the oven to 350°F (175°C). Brush each financier cavity or individual pan with a little soft butter.

6. Pipe the batter into each financier pan until it is three-quarters full. Top each one with a few chopped hazelnuts.

7. Bake for 8 minutes for small or 12 minutes for larger financers, until golden brown and a toothpick inserted into the center comes out clean, or with a little crumb. Let cool for several minutes before removing them from the pan or they may break.

8. Store in an airtight container for up to 3 days.

Variations

You can use any sort of nut flour, such as hazelnut, almond, or pistachio, for different versions.

Madame Madeleine

Here's the quick story on this delicate pastry and how it became so emblematic of French pastry: In 1755, King Stanislaus of Poland back was hosting Voltaire and several other important people, so he asked his pastry chef, Madeleine, to bake something special. He then sent a batch to his daughter, Marie, wife to Louis XV. She fell completely in love with them and decided to name them madeleines in the chef's honor.

Yield: 12 full-size madeleines

Prep Time: 10 minutes

Rest Time: 9–15 hours

Bake Time: 15 minutes

Difficulty: Easy

Tools: Stand mixer, rubber spatula, madeleines pan, piping bag, pastry brush

---

80 g (⅓ cup) granulated sugar

100 g (2) eggs, at room temperature

20 g (1 tablespoon) honey

Zest of 2 lemons

9 g (2 teaspoons) pure vanilla extract

100 g (¾ cup) all-purpose flour, plus more for the pan

10 g (2 teaspoons) baking powder

113 g (½ cup) unsalted butter, plus more for the pan

Powdered sugar, for dusting

Chef Tips

The thermal shock of the cold pan going into the very hot oven creates that iconic hump in the center. Use a metal pan, not a silicone pan, for the best results and to get a nice crisp exterior and soft sponge on the inside.

1. In a stand mixer fitted with a whisk attachment, combine the granulated sugar, eggs, honey, lemon zest, and vanilla. Whisk for about 10 minutes until the mixture is thickened and doubled in size. This is the most important part of the recipe. The eggs should be almost at the ribbon stage (page 22).

2. In a separate bowl, combine the flour and baking powder. Whisk to combine.

3. In a small saucepan, melt the butter and set aside.

4. Once the egg mixture is ready, use a rubber spatula to fold in the dry ingredients delicately, so as not to deflate the eggs. Alternate adding 8–16 g (1–2 tablespoons) of the flour mix and some of the melted butter until smooth. Load into a piping bag and chill in the refrigerator for a minimum of 6 hours, preferably 12 hours.

5. Brush the madeleine pan with butter and dust with flour. Place the pan in the freezer and chill for at least 3 hours. Chill the pan overnight while the batter is in the refrigerator so by morning they are both ready to go.

6. When ready to bake, preheat the oven to 410°F (210°C).

7. Pipe the batter into each madeleine pan hole until it is three-quarters full. Bake for 10–15 minutes, or until golden brown. Do not open the oven during the first 10 minutes to get the iconic hump in the center of your madeleine.

8. Allow the madeleines to cool for 5–10 minutes before removing them from the pan or they will stick and break.

9. These can dry out quickly, so dust with a little powdered sugar and store in an airtight container for up to 3 days.

Variations

* Feel free to use orange zest or even coffee extract to try out other fun flavors. To make a chocolaty version, replace 20 g (2½ tablespoons) of flour with 20 g (2½ tablespoons) of cocoa powder.
* You can also dip these into some melted chocolate, place on parchment paper, and allow the chocolate to set up to create a crunchy chocolate shell on the outside.

Raspberry Blossom Almond Cake Bites

These small cakes taste like an almond financier with baked raspberries in the center, only this one is easier to make because we don't need to make brown butter. This recipe comes together quickly and is sure to delight any guests who walks through the door. These look like you picked them up in a chic French bakery, but, secretly, they only take 15 minutes to put together. It will be our little secret. The freshness of the berries is essential to the success of this dessert.

Yield: 12 small cakes

Prep Time: 15 minutes

Bake Time: 20 minutes

Difficulty: Easy

Tools: Stand mixer, rubber spatula, cupcake pan, piping bag, pastry brush

240 g (2 cups) almond flour

20 g (2½ tablespoons) all-purpose flour

120 g (1 cup) powdered sugar

130 g (½ cup + 1 tablespoon) unsalted butter, at room temperature

200 g (4) eggs, at room temperature

8 g (2 teaspoons) vanilla bean paste

4 g (1 teaspoon) almond extract

60 small raspberries

60 g (¾ cup) sliced almonds, for topping

80 g (¼ cup) raspberry jam, for topping

1. Preheat the oven to 375°F (190°C). Brush each cupcake pan generously with butter (no need to dust them with flour) or use cupcake liners.

2. In a stand mixer fitted with a paddle attachment, add the almond flour, all-purpose flour, and powdered sugar. Mix to combine.

3. Place the butter in a microwave-safe bowl and melt for 20–30 seconds, until *almost* fully melted. Stream the butter into the flour mixture. Mix together until smooth, 2 minutes. Add the eggs one at a time, mixing on medium speed in between each egg. Add the vanilla bean paste and almond extract and mix for 2 minutes until smooth. Load into a piping bag and set aside.

4. Pipe an even amount of batter into each cavity of the cupcake pan roughly three-quarters of the way full. Gently push 3 raspberries into each one. Crumble some sliced almond pieces on top of each one.

5. Place the cupcake pan on a baking sheet and place on the center rack. Bake for 17–20 minutes, until the edges are golden brown and the top is slightly golden brown or until a toothpick inserted into the center comes out almost clean, with just a few crumbs.

6. Remove from the oven and let cool for 10 minutes before removing the cake bites from the pan. Use a small paring knife to help you prop them out.

7. For the finishing touch, in a small bowl, add the raspberry jam. Heat in the microwave for 20 seconds to get it nice and liquidly.

8. Sprinkle each cake with a few more sliced almonds. Dip the remaining raspberries in the jam and then use them to decorate each almond cake. Place two on the top of each cake.

9. These will stay nice and shiny for several hours before serving. Keep them in an airtight container at room temperature for up to 2 days. If you don't decorate each one with the fresh raspberries until serving them, you can keep the cakes for up to 4 days.

Variations

I would not recommend using frozen fruit or berries because they will release too much moisture. However, try different fresh berries, like blueberries or strawberries. For added flavor, you can toast the almonds at 350°F (175°C) for 15 minutes to get them a little golden.

Coconut Scone Brunch Bites

These scones are one of my favorite recipes. They mix up quickly in one bowl and are a great way to use up those old blueberries, strawberries, or even chopped apples. I am often asked why there is no butter in this recipe. The answer is it simply does not need it. We are looking to create a cakelike crumb texture. The crunchy crust on the outside from the brown sugar topping keeps these super soft in the middle, and is the secret to these perfect scones.

Yield: 22 small or 11 large scones

Prep Time: 10 minutes

Bake Time: 15 minutes or
25 minutes (depending on size)

Difficulty: Easy

Tools: Rubber Stand mixer, spatula, silicone mat

For the Scones

360 g (3 cups) all-purpose flour

60 g (⅓ cup) granulated sugar

11 g (1 tablespoon) baking powder

360 g (1½ cups) crème fraîche or sour cream

100 g (¾ cup) dark chocolate chips

100 g (¾ cup) milk chocolate chips

120 g (1⅔ cups) shredded unsweetened coconut

For the Sugar Crust

60 g (¼ cup) crème fraîche or sour cream

200 g (1 cup) light brown sugar

Chef Tips

Before brushing the scones with the crème fraîche, allow them to rest at room temperature or in the refrigerator for an hour before baking to allow the gluten in the flour to relax ONLY if the dough is sticky; this will give you a much nicer crumb result. If it's a "get these on the table quick" kind of day, they will still be delicious if baked right away. Do not use dark brown sugar in place of light brown sugar, or the scone bites will get too dark on the outside.

1. Preheat the oven to 350°F (175°C). Line a baking sheet with a silicone mat or parchment paper.

2. To make the scones: In a stand mixer fitted with a paddle attachment, add the flour, granulated sugar, and baking powder and mix for 2 minutes just to combine.

3. Add the crème fraîche and mix for 2 minutes, just until all the flour is absorbed and the dough forms a nice ball. DO NOT overmix this dough or it will become stretchy and wet and very tough. If this happens, simply place the bowl in the refrigerator and chill for 2 hours. Add the chocolate chips and dried coconut and mix to combine.

4. Weigh each scone on a baking scale to ensure all of them weigh the same. If you don't have a scale, tear off even-size pieces by hand and then roll each scone into a tight ball. Place on the prepared baking sheet. Space them out evenly for proper airflow.

5. To make the sugar crust: Coat each scone with a little bit of crème fraîche on the outside. Place the brown sugar in a bowl and dunk each scone in the sugar. Get an even coating all the way around. Place on the baking sheet and bake for 15–25 minutes, depending on the size, until golden brown.

6. Slide the silicone mat off the baking sheet without touching the scones to stop the baking process. Allow them to cool to room temperature.

7. Store the scones in an airtight container at room temperature for up to 1 week. I do not recommend freezing these.

Variations

You can substitute the crème fraîche for sour cream or Greek yogurt. When substituting the "additions," be sure to add back the exact same weight so as not to alter the recipe. You can use 320 g (11½ oz) of nuts and fresh berries in place of the chocolate chips and coconut.

Chocolate Fondant Cake Bites

A chocolate fondant is a small French cake that is somewhere between a flourless chocolate cake and a lava cake in terms of texture. It is a very rich and chocolaty dense crumb with a soft molten center. This recipe also uses one of my favorite ingredients: sweet chestnut cream, which I could eat out of the jar.

Yield: 12 mini cakes

Prep Time: 10 minutes

Bake Time: 20 minutes

Difficulty: Easy

Tools: Stand mixer, cupcake pan, pastry brush

---

250 g (1½ cups) dark chocolate chips

113 g (½ cup) unsalted butter, at room temperature

200 g (⅔ cup) sweet chestnut cream

60 g (3) egg yolks, at room temperature

25 g (¼ cup) all-purpose flour

Chef Tips

The key to this recipe is almost underbaking it a minute or two to keep that soft gooey center.

1. Preheat the oven to 325°F (160°C). Brush each cavity of a cupcake pan with butter and lightly dust with flour, tapping out the excess.

2. In a microwave-safe bowl, add the chocolate chips and butter. Heat for 30 seconds until the butter is fully melted and coating the chocolate chips. Let stand for 20 seconds and then whisk to combine until smooth and shiny. Add the chestnut cream and whisk for 2 minutes until smooth. Add the yolks one at a time, mixing in between each addition. Add the flour and whisk to combine. Transfer the batter to a piping bag without a piping tip.

3. Pipe the batter into each cavity until all are about three-quarters full. Place on a baking sheet and transfer to the center rack of the oven. Bake for 17–20 minutes. The edges of the cakes should pull away from the pan, but the center of each cake should still look underdone and gooey.

4. Let cool to room temperature and unmold the cakes using a paring knife to help you pop them out. Store in an airtight container at room temperature for up to 4 days, or store the batter in the refrigerator for up to 1 week and bake fresh every day.

Chouquettes Chérie

Pâte à choux is an iconic French pastry recipe, used to make St. Honoré, éclairs, religieuse, croquembouche, and so many others. Chouquettes are hollow choux puffs covered in pearl sugar and a little simple syrup. They make the perfect bite for breakfast, tea, or an afternoon snack.

Yield: 20–25 choux

Prep Time: 15–20 minutes

Bake Time: 20–25 minutes

Difficulty: Intermediate

Tools: Rubber spatula, piping bag, pastry brush

1 batch Pâte à Choux Dough (page 38), unbaked

150 g (5½ oz) pearl sugar crystals (topping)

For the Egg Wash

50 g (1) egg

15 ml (1 tablespoon) heavy cream

5 g (1 teaspoon) granulated sugar

½ batch Simple Syrup (page 61)

1. Line two baking sheets with parchment paper or silicone mats.

2. Pipe the choux into small dollops spaced out evenly on the baking sheets so they don't stick together. Try to pipe them to an even count in your head for rhythm.

3. Make the egg wash. Combine the egg, heavy cream, and sugar. Brush each choux with a small amount of egg wash.

4. Pour the pearl sugar generously over the top of each one so they are coated. A lot of the sugar will fall off during the baking process.

5. Preheat the oven to 350°F (175°C).

6. Bake each sheet one at a time so they do not overlap in the oven until dark golden brown, 15–20 minutes. DO NOT open the oven in the first 15 minutes. As soon as the pastries come out of the oven and are still warm, brush each one with a little simple syrup. Allow them to cool on the baking sheet.

7. If you would like to keep some of these frozen, don't brush them with simple syrup. To freeze them, simply wait for them to cool and place them in an airtight freezer bag. When you are ready to eat them, preheat the oven 350°F (175°C), and bake from frozen for 3–4 minutes, then brush with the simple syrup and serve right away.

8. Store the chouquettes in an airtight container at room temperature for up to 3 days. These are best enjoyed fresh.

Raspberry Cinnamon Nonnettes

Nonnettes, roughly translated in French, means "little nuns." This dessert is often served during the holiday season. It originated in the region of Dijon, France, in 1796 when nuns at the abbey started creating different versions of the cakes that were sold to the public. The texture and flavor of this cake is very similar to that of gingerbread, with a dense, moist crumb and a lot of honey and spices. I wanted to create a fun variation using honey, raspberry jam, and cinnamon, but feel free to make it your own.

Yield: 12 mini cakes

Prep Time: 10 minutes

Bake Time: 20–25 minutes

Difficulty: Easy

Tools: Stand mixer, rubber spatula, cupcake pan

For the Nonnettes

100 ml (⅓ cup) whole milk

2 cinnamon sticks

2 g (½ teaspoon) ground cinnamon

175 g (1½ cups) all-purpose flour

15 g (2 tablespoons) cornstarch

13 g (1 tablespoon) baking powder

250 g (¾ cup) raspberry jam

230 g (⅔ cup) honey

100 g (2) eggs, at room temperature

113 g (½ cup) unsalted butter, at room temperature

For the Glaze

60 g (¼ cup) raspberry jam

21 g (1 tablespoon) honey

Chef Tips

I recommend using a high-quality jam that is not full of sugar. Use one with lots of fruit and flavor, as it is the highlight ingredient in this recipe and essential to the wonderfully soft texture.

1. Preheat the oven 350°F (175°C). Brush each cavity of a cupcake pan with butter and lightly dust with flour, then tap out the excess flour.

2. To make the nonnettes: In a 3- or 4-qt (2.7- or 3.6-l) saucepan, add the milk, cinnamon sticks, and cinnamon. Bring to a boil over high heat, remove from the heat, cover, and let sit for 10 minutes to infuse the spices into the milk.

3. In a stand mixer with a paddle attachment, add the flour, cornstarch, and baking powder. Mix together for 1 minute to combine. Add the jam and honey and mix for about 2 minutes, until the batter is nice and smooth.

4. Add the eggs one at time. Mix for 1 minute in between each addition to keep the batter nice and smooth. Finally, add the butter. It should be very soft so that it incorporates easily into the batter. If you still see some visible lumps, use a whisk to help smooth out the batter.

5. Remove the cinnamon sticks from the milk and pour it over the batter as you whisk to combine. The batter should be complexly smooth. Pour the batter into each cavity using a piping bag or an ice cream scooper until about three-quarters full. Place the cupcake pan on a baking sheet.

6. Transfer to the oven on the center rack and bake for 20–25 minutes, or until a toothpick inserted into the center comes out almost completely clean. Allow the nonnettes to cool before unmolding them so they don't stick.

7. To make the glaze: Combine the jam and honey in a small microwave-safe bowl and heat in the microwave for 20 seconds. Mix together and brush over the top of each nonnette. This will give them a really nice shine and finish. It will also keep them softer longer.

8. Store the nonnettes in an airtight container at room temperature for up to 4 days.

Helenettes

This chewy almond cookie comes together very easily and is one of my favorites to always have on hand by the espresso machine. It is similar to the Italian amaretti cookie in texture—chewy with a slightly crispy exterior. It's also delicious if you use hazelnut flour instead of the almond flour for a nuttier and richer flavor.

Yield: 18 cookies (25 g [1 oz]) each

Prep Time: 20 minutes

Bake Time: 12–13 minutes

Difficulty: Easy

Tools: Stand mixer, silicone mat, rubber spatula

---

60 g (3) egg yolks, at room temperature

50 g (½ cup) powdered sugar

50 g (¼ cup) granulated sugar

4 g (1 teaspoon) vanilla bean paste

2 g (½ teaspoon) almond extract

80 g (⅓ cup) unsalted butter, melted

100 g (¾ cup) all-purpose flour

120 g (1¼ cups) almond flour

100 g (¾ cup) whole toasted almonds, for topping

Chef Tips

Take the time to roll these into balls, and weighing each individually to get perfectly shaped cookies. This ensures they will all bake in the same amount of time.

1. Preheat the oven to 375°F (190°C). Line a baking sheet with a silicone mat or parchment paper.

2. In a stand mixer fitted with a whisk attachment or in a mixing bowl with a whisk, add the egg yolks, powdered sugar, granulated sugar, vanilla bean paste, and almond extract. Whisk for 10 minutes until thick and pale in color and doubled in volume. When you take a tiny amount in between two fingers you should no longer feel any of the sugar granules.

3. Stream in the melted butter (careful to have it melted but not hot) and continue to whisk on low speed for 2 minutes until fully incorporated and smooth.

4. In a small bowl, mix together the all-purpose flour and almond flour. Gently fold in the flour mixture into the egg mixture using a rubber spatula. Combine until smooth. There is no baking powder in the recipe, so try not to deflate the eggs to keep a nice chewy texture in the cookies.

5. Using a scale, spoon out small amounts of the cookie dough. Each cookie should weigh 25 g (1 oz). Roll each one into a perfect ball and place all of them on the prepared baking sheet, leaving room in between each one for proper airflow. Gently flatten each ball slightly and place an almond in the center of each cookie.

6. Bake for 12–13 minutes, until lightly golden brown and firm. The bottom of each cookie should also be lightly golden brown.

7. Slide the baking mat off of the baking sheet without disturbing the cookies to stop the baking process. Allow the cookies to cool completely. Store in an airtight container for up to 1 week.

Variations

You can easily substitute the weight of the almond flour with any other nut flour you like. Hazelnut or pistachio is absolutely delicious as well. For a little added sweet touch, you can melt some dark chocolate in a bain-marie (double boiler) or in a microwave-safe bowl and dip the bottom of each cookie into the chocolate. Place the cookies on a sheet of parchment paper and allow the chocolate to set, then store in an airtight container.

Diamond Cookies
(Sablés Diamant)

The texture of this cookie lies somewhere between a shortbread cookie and a sugar cookie. It is very delicate and so delicious. My nieces love this one because it is sparkly from the sugar crystals on the outside, giving it the name "diamond cookie." I think we should all have a reliable simple cookie recipe in our repertoire to turn any ordinary coffee break into a moment of pure delicious joy.

Yield: 24–30 cookies (depending on thickness)

Prep Time: 10 minutes

Bake Time: 15 minutes

Difficulty: Easy

Tools: Stand mixer, rubber spatula, silicone mat, pastry brush, chef's knife

180 g (¾ cup) unsalted butter, at room temperature

80 g (¾ cup) powdered sugar

4 g (1 teaspoon) vanilla bean paste

50 g (1) egg, at room temperature

250 g (2 cups) all-purpose flour

For the Diamond Topping

30 g (1) egg white, at room temperature

220 g (1 cup) raw sugar crystals

1. In a stand mixer fitted with a paddle attachment or a mixing bowl with a spatula, add the butter, powdered sugar, and vanilla. Beat on medium speed for 5 minutes. Scrape down the sides of the bowl and whip for 2 minutes longer. The mixture should be pale in color and fluffy. Add the egg and mix for 5 minutes on medium speed. Add the flour all at once and whip on low speed for 2 minutes. The dough should be stiff and hold together.

2. Divide the dough into 2 large balls. Shape each one into a 2- to 3-inch (5- to 7.5-cm) thick log using plastic wrap underneath to help you shape it and keep it from sticking to the work surface. If the dough is a little soft or sticky, place the logs wrapped in plastic wrap in the refrigerator for 2 hours. If the dough is not sticky, simply refrigerate for 20 minutes.

3. When ready to bake, preheat the oven to 325°F (160°C). Line two baking sheets with silicone mats or parchment paper.

4. To make the diamond topping: Brush each log with a little egg white to use as the "glue." Pour the raw sugar crystals onto a plate and roll the logs on the sugar until fully coated. Using a chef's knife, slice the logs ¼ inch (6 mm) thick. Place the cookies on the prepared baking sheets, spacing them out about ½ inch (1.3 cm) apart in offset lines.

5. Bake the cookies for 12–15 minutes, until golden brown on the bottom and around the edges; the center of the cookie will stay nice and white. Allow the cookies to come to room temperature before storing them in an airtight container for up to 2 weeks.

6. If you would like to bake these from frozen to keep on hand, simply store the cookie dough logs in the plastic wrap *without* the egg white and sugar crystals. To bake from frozen, transfer the logs to the refrigerator a few hours in advance, then proceed from Step 3.

Chocolate Salami
(Saucisson au Chocolat)

If you have never made this recipe before, you are in for a very fun treat. This dessert mimics a salami with the chocolate rolled up and dusted in powdered sugar. It is so delicious and so much fun to make. You can use almost any ingredients you have on hand. This is also a very popular dessert to bring to dinners during the holiday season. Think rocky road, but in log form.

Yield: 20 slices

Prep Time: 15 minutes

Chill Time: 2 hours

Difficulty: Easy

Tools: Rubber spatula, chef's knife, butcher's twine

---

100 g (3½ oz) cat's tongue cookies or other butter cookies (page 99)

25 g (¼ cup) shelled whole unsalted pistachios

25 g (¼ cup) dried cranberries

25 g (2 tablespoons) chopped hazelnuts

20 mini marshmallows

200 g (1¼ cups) dark chocolate chips

50 g (⅓ cup) milk chocolate chips

113 g (½ cup) unsalted butter, at room temperature

40 g (⅓ cup) powdered sugar, for dusting

1. Break the butter cookies into bite-size pieces and place in a large bowl. Add the pistachios, dried cranberries, hazelnuts, and mini marshmallows.

2. In a microwave-safe bowl, add the dark chocolate chips, milk chocolate chips, and butter. Melt in the microwave for 25 seconds. Mix gently to combine. If not completely melted, heat for 25 seconds and finish mixing. The chocolate should be completely smooth.

3. Pour the chocolate mixture over the cookie mixture. Mix together to make sure everything is completely coated in chocolate.

4. Lay out a piece of plastic wrap on your work surface. Pour half of the chocolate mixture on it and roll into a nice tight log. Repeat the same process for the other half of the mixture. Chill the logs in the refrigerator for at least 2 hours.

5. Once the logs are firm, remove from the plastic wrap and dust with powdered sugar for the perfect salami effect. For that final touch, you can wrap each "salami" with butcher's twine to make it look even more real.

6. Store in the refrigerator for up to 2 weeks and serve cold or at room temperature on a cutting board for a fun and easy dessert.

Chuffins

Welcome to one of the simplest recipes in the book, but also one of the most delicious. This churro/muffin hybrid has the perfect amount of sweetness from the cinnamon sugar and is the perfect treat for snack time or even breakfast. Try adding some mini chocolate chips for a different version.

Yield: 24 mini or 12 full-size chuffins

Prep Time: 10 minutes

Bake Time: 15–20 minutes . . . . . .
(depending on size)

Difficulty: Easy

Tools: Stand mixer, rubber spatula, cupcake pan, piping bag, pastry brush

For the Muffins

50 g (¼ cup) granulated sugar

50 g (¼ cup) dark brown sugar

120 g (1 cup) all-purpose flour

10 g (2 teaspoons) baking powder

113 g (½ cup) unsalted butter, melted

120 ml (½ cup) whole milk, plus more as needed, at room temperature

4.5 g (1 teaspoon) pure vanilla extract

For the Churro Bath

113 g (½ cup) unsalted butter

100 g (½ cup) granulated sugar

10 g (2 teaspoons) ground cinnamon

Chef Tips

Allow the chuffins to cool slightly before unmolding them to avoid breaking, brushing them with butter, and dipping the in the churro sugar bath to prevent the cake from absorbing all the butter.

1. Preheat the oven to 350°F (175°C). Grease a mini or full-size muffin pan with generous amounts of butter spray or brush with soft butter.

2. To make the muffins: In a mixing bowl with a spatula or in a stand mixer fitted with a paddle attachment, add the granulated sugar, brown sugar, flour, and baking powder and mix to combine.

3. In a separate bowl, combine the melted butter, milk, and vanilla. Work with milk at room temperature or the butter will solidify. Pour over the flour mixture and fold together to form the batter. If the batter is a little stiff, add an extra 15–30 g (1–2 tablespoons) of milk. Transfer to a piping bag without a tip.

4. Pipe even amounts of the batter into each cavity in the prepared muffin pan and bake for 15–20 minutes, until lightly golden brown around the edges and a toothpick inserted into the center of a muffin comes out almost clean, with a few crumbs. Allow the muffins to cool slightly, and then remove from the pan.

5. To make the churro bath: In a microwave-safe bowl, melt the butter. In a small bowl, combine the granulated sugar and cinnamon. Brush each muffin with melted butter and dip them in the bowl of cinnamon sugar.

6. Store in an airtight container for the best flavor and consistency for up to 3 days.

Variations
Add chocolate chips or fill with a little jam once they've cooled for a donut effect or dust them in powdered sugar instead.

Meringue Kisses

Meringues are made with sugar and egg whites. Here we are making an
Italian meringue, which keeps these little babies nice and shiny.
These are wonderful to eat as they are or to use as decoration on cakes.

Yield: 40–50 mini meringues

Prep Time: 15 minutes

Bake Time: 4–6 hours

Difficulty: Intermediate

Tools: Stand mixer, piping bag, round piping tip, silicone mat

250 g (1¼ cups) granulated sugar

60 ml (¼ cup) water

20 g (1 tablespoon) glucose or corn syrup

120 g (4) egg whites, at room temperature

Chef Tips

See Meringue 101 on page 24 for a refresher on all the tips and tricks to make the perfect meringues. Always use eggs at room temperature for the best results and use aged egg whites to create the shiniest meringues.

1. Preheat the oven to the lowest setting, around 200°F (95°C). Line two baking sheets with silicone mats or parchment paper.

2. In a 2- or 3-qt (1.8- or 2.7-l) saucepan, add the sugar, water, and glucose. Make sure all of the sugar is coated in water so it cooks evenly and does not stick to the bottom of the pot. Cook over medium heat, *without stirring*, until a candy thermometer registers 250°F (120°C), the soft crack stage. If you don't have a thermometer, pour a tiny amount of sugar into an ice cold glass of water. If the sugar is firm, it is ready; if it dissolves, keep cooking and test again.

3. While the sugar syrup is cooking, place the egg whites in a stand mixer fitted with a whisk attachment. Begin whisking on medium speed to get the egg whites nice and frothy. Stream in the sugar syrup slowly as you continue to whisk the egg whites. Whisk for 10 minutes longer until stiff peaks form and the bowl is cool to the touch.

4. Transfer the meringue to a piping bag. You can use a small round tip or simply pipe right out of the bag. Pipe the meringues onto the prepared baking sheets. Keep a rhythm in your head as you are piping to make even and consistent meringue kisses.

5. Transfer the baking sheets to the oven. Dehydrate the meringues until they are completely dry, about 4 hours. This will keep them white and shiny. If you use a higher oven temperature, they will bake much faster and become light golden brown instead of staying perfectly white.

6. Store in an airtight container at room temperature for up to 1 month.

Mini Palmier Hearts

Is there anything better than delicate little hearts of crispy puff pastry caramelized with sugar? These are often an after-school snack in Paris. They come in two sizes and are sometimes dipped in chocolate. They also make wonderful savory snacks when baked with cheese or tomato paste and basil. These come together quickly with a rough puff pastry or your favorite store-bought brand.

Yield: 30–40 mini palmiers

Prep Time: 15 minutes

Chill Time: 20 minutes

Bake Time: 15–20 minutes

Difficulty: Intermediate

Tools: Silicone mats, chef's knife, rolling pin, offset spatula

100 g (½ cup) granulated sugar

1 sheet Rough Puff Pastry (page 33) or store-bought

30 g (¼ cup) powdered sugar, for dusting

1. Dust your work surface with half of the granulated sugar. Place the puff pastry sheet on top and roll it out slightly to absorb the sugar into the dough, maintaining that rectangular shape. Flip it upside down and dust the other side with the remaining granulated sugar.

2. Place the puff pastry sheet lengthwise in front of you. Fold both sides toward the center. Sprinkle some of the granulated sugar left on the work surface and fold over again toward the center until both sides meet in the middle. Place the heart log in the freezer for 20 minutes.

3. When ready to bake, preheat the oven 375°F (190°C). Line two baking sheets with silicone mats or parchment paper. Here, silicone mats really help get a more caramelized coloring.

4. Remove the log from the freezer and use a sharp chef's knife to cut the log into slices ¼ inch (6 mm) thick. Place the little hearts on the prepared baking sheets and space them out evenly so they have room to finish expanding in the oven. Dust all the hearts with powdered sugar. You will dust them again after you flip them over.

 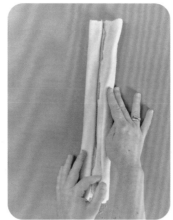 

5. Bake one sheet at a time on the center rack for 10 minutes. Store the other baking sheet in the freezer until ready to bake. Quickly slide the sheet out of the oven and flip the hearts over using an offset spatula. Dust this side with powdered sugar and place back in the oven for 7–8 minutes longer. They will be golden brown and a little darker around the edges than the middle. Remove from the oven and let cool to room temperature.

6. Store in an airtight container for up to 3 days. Store the unbaked log in the freezer wrapped in parchment and plastic wrap for up to 1 month.

Variations

Add cinnamon sugar or dip the hearts in chocolate once cooled. For a savory option, you can brush the sheet with butter and sprinkle with Gruyère cheese. These pastries make for a perfect aperitif or mini hors d'oeuvre.

Cat's Tongue Cookies
(Langues de Chat)

This sweet, light, and delicate biscuit is really unique in both taste and texture. It is crispy but melts in your mouth at the same time. In Paris, a lot of high-end restaurants serve these with the check at the end of a meal. You can make them in almost any flavor you want. Using top-quality vanilla is a must. These are wonderful to keep in an airtight container next to the espresso machine.

Yield: About 50 cookies

Prep Time: 10 minutes

Bake Time: 15–20 minutes

Difficulty: Easy

Tools: Stand mixer, rubber spatula, piping bag

130 g (½ cup) unsalted butter, at room temperature

160 g (1½ cups) powdered sugar

4 g (1 teaspoon) pure vanilla extract or 1 vanilla bean, split and scraped

60 g (2) egg whites, at room temperature

160 g (1¼ cups) all-purpose flour

20 ml (4 teaspoons) whole milk, at room temperature

Chef Tips

If the batter is a little too soft to pipe, simply cover it with plastic wrap and place in the refrigerator for 1 hour before baking. You can also keep this batter for several days in the refrigerator and bake these off fresh every morning.

1. Preheat the oven to 325°F (160°C). Line two or three baking sheets with parchment paper and trace 3-inch (7.5-cm) vertical lines equally spaced 1 inch (2.5 cm) apart. Flip the paper upside down and use as a stencil to pipe small sticks of batter.

2. In a mixing bowl with a spatula or in a stand mixer fitted with a paddle attachment, add the butter. This is the most important part of the recipe. The butter should be pommade consistency, like lotion, very spreadable and soft but not melted at all. Add the powdered sugar and vanilla extract or seeds and mix to combine. Add the egg whites one at a time, mixing in between each addition for 2–3 minutes to get everything combined and perfectly smooth. There should be no lumps.

3. Add the flour all at once. Mix on low speed for 2–3 minutes. Scrape down the sides of the bowl, add the milk, and mix for 1 minute longer. The batter should be perfectly smooth.

4. Transfer the batter to a piping bag fitted with a small round tip. If you don't have one, you can pipe these without the tip. Pipe small sticks onto the prepared baking sheets following the lines. They will spread a little as they bake. Bake for 15–20 minutes, until ONLY the edges are golden brown. The center of the cookie will stay nice and white.

5. Let cool to room temperature and store in an airtight container in a dry place at room temperature for up to 2 weeks.

Variations

These are great dipped in chocolate. You can also make a chocolate version by removing 20 g (¾ oz) of flour and substituting with 20 g (¾ oz) of cocoa powder. If you are a coffee fan, add half a shot of espresso (15 ml, or 1 tablespoon). I've also made these with chopped dark chocolate in the batter, which creates a zebra effect.

Lemon Meringue Choux

This delicate choux is filled with lemon curd and topped with a crunchy layer of craquelin and creamy Italian meringue. This one hits every mark on the tasting charts. The tart lemon curd perfectly balances the sweet meringue. It's an elegant French pastry that tastes like sunshine in every bite. Store the choux in the freezer and whip these up for the next barbecue or event of the season for an elegant touch.

Yield: 18–20 choux puffs

Prep Time: 25 minutes

Difficulty: Intermediate

Tools: Rubber spatula or wooden spoon, kitchen torch, piping bags

1 batch Pâte à Choux with craquelin layer, baked in 2-inch rounds (page 82)

For the Lemon Curd

200 g (4) eggs,
  at room temperature

80 g (4) egg yolks,
  at room temperature

112 g (½ cup) granulated sugar

80 g (⅔ cup) all-purpose flour

60 ml (¼ cup) fresh lemon juice

Zest of 2 lemons, plus more
  for garnish

227 g (1 cup) unsalted butter,
  cubed, at room temperature

1 batch Italian meringue
  (see Meringue Kisses, page 94)

1. To make the lemon curd: In a 3- or 4-qt (2.7- or 3.6-l) saucepan, add about 235 ml (1 cup) of water to create a double boiler. In a mixing bowl that fits on top of the pan, add the eggs, egg yolks, and sugar. Whisk together for 2–3 minutes, until slightly frothy and combined. Turn on the heat to medium, add the flour, lemon juice, and lemon zest and whisk to combine.

2. Switch to a rubber spatula or wooden spoon and cook over medium heat for 10–12 minutes, until thickened, mixing continuously so as not to curdle your eggs. The mixture should coat the back of the spatula. Trace a line in the curd on the spatula; if the mixture drips, covering the line, it needs a few minutes longer. If you have a straight line the curd is perfectly thickened. Remove from the heat, cover right away with plastic wrap to prevent a skin from forming on top of the curd, and let cool for 10 minutes.

3. Uncover the curd. Add the butter one piece at a time, mixing with a whisk in between each addition. Make sure the butter is soft and at room temperature so it is easier to incorporate. The butter creates a very creamy lemon curd, so take your time incorporating it slowly.

4. Cover the bowl with plastic wrap, with the plastic touching the curd to prevent any air contact, and reserve in the refrigerator.

5. To assemble: Slice off the top of each choux. Pipe a small amount of lemon curd into each one. Pipe some of the Italian meringue on top of each choux. Brown with a kitchen torch for a toasted look. Top with the little hat you cut off earlier. Garnish with a pinch of lemon zest and serve right away. These cannot be saved or stored for later, because the choux will soften from the moistness of the lemon curd and meringue. However, to prep these for an event, make the choux puffs ahead of time and store them in the freezer until ready to assemble. The lemon curd can also be made several days in advance.

Mini Cookie Cereal

This is a nostalgic recipe for my '90s friends. Do you remember having crispy cookie cereal for breakfast and drinking that delicious milk afterward? Well, now you can enjoy a much tastier gourmet version without any additives or preservatives. These are a labor of love; they are easy to make, but take a little time to pipe. You can make a big batch and keep them for several weeks.

Yield: 100 bite-size cookies

Prep Time: 10 minutes

Bake Time: 15 minutes

Difficulty: Easy

Tools: Stand mixer, piping bag, rubber spatula, silicone mat

227 g (1 cup) unsalted butter, at room temperature

150 g (¾ cup) light brown sugar

100 g (½ cup) granulated sugar

4 g (1 teaspoon) vanilla bean paste

50 g (1) egg, at room temperature

20 g (1) egg yolk, at room temperature

250 g (2⅛ cups) all-purpose flour

10 g (2 teaspoons) baking powder

180 g (¾ cup) mini chocolate chips

Chef Tips

These bake up quickly because they're so tiny, so keep an eye on them to avoid burning them. Set a timer! Regular-size chips are too big for these cookies, so you really want to use the minis.

1. Preheat the oven to 350°F (175°C). Line a few baking sheets with silicone mats or parchment paper.

2. In a mixing bowl with a spatula by hand or in a stand mixer fitted with a paddle attachment, add the butter, brown sugar, and granulated sugar. Beat on medium speed for about 5 minutes, until creamy and pale in color. Add the vanilla and beat for 2–3 minutes until fluffy. Add the egg and beat for 2 minutes. Scrape down the sides of the bowl and add the egg yolk. Beat to combine and keep the mixture nice and smooth.

3. Add the flour and baking powder all at once. Mix on low speed to incorporate the dry ingredients, being careful not to overmix the dough. You just need the dough to form together and absorb all the flour. Add the mini chocolate chips. Mix on low speed for 1 minute to combine. Transfer the cookie dough to a piping bag.

4. Pipe nickel-size cookies onto the prepared baking sheets, squeezing at the bottom of the bag every 2 seconds to pipe consistently and get the same size cookies.

5. Bake for 10 minutes, or until the cookies are golden brown. Be careful because these are very small and bake very quickly. If the cookies are really small, they may only take 8 minutes. Transfer to a wire rack and let cool to room temperature before removing them from the parchment paper or silicone mat.

6. Store in an airtight container for up to 2 weeks. Enjoy in cold milk, chocolate milk, or yogurt.

Waffle Sticks with Maple Butter

Level up your next brunch with these adorable waffle sticks. Crispy on the outside and soft in the center, they are the perfect sweet bite without being overpowering, and everything is cuter when it's in miniature. . This book has a series of classic American recipes that I am obsessed with. Because I have dual nationality (American and French), my desserts are often influenced by both cultures. The whipped maple butter makes for the perfect pairing of a salty-sweet dunking topping.

Yield: 40–50 mini waffle sticks

Prep Time: 15 minutes

Bake Time: 6–8 minutes

Difficulty: Easy

Tools: Waffle stick pan, stand mixer, balloon whisk, piping bag, rubber spatula

For the Waffles

180 g (1½ cups) all-purpose flour

12 g (2½ teaspoons) baking powder

Pinch of salt

60 g (⅓ cup) granulated sugar

115 ml (½ cup) whole milk, at room temperature

100 g (2) eggs, at room temperature

9 g (2 teaspoons) vanilla bean paste

35 ml (2½ tablespoons) grapeseed oil or neutral oil

For the Whipped Maple Butter

113 g (½ cup) unsalted butter, at room temperature

40 ml (2 tablespoons + 2 teaspoons) maple syrup

25 g (¼ cup) powdered sugar

45 ml (3 tablespoons) whole milk or heavy cream, at room temperature

2 g (¼ teaspoon) flaky sea salt

1. Preheat the oven to 375°F (190°C). Brush a waffle stick pan with melted butter or oil.

2. To make the waffles: Make sure your ingredients are at room temperature. In a mixing bowl or stand mixer fitted with paddle attachment, add the flour, baking powder, salt, and granulated sugar. Mix to combine.

3. In a separate bowl, whisk together the milk, eggs, vanilla, and oil for 1 minute. As you whisk by hand or with the mixer at low speed, stream the wet ingredients into the dry ingredients to form a batter. If you have lumps, use a whisk to help break them up. Set aside and allow to rest 15 minutes.

4. Pipe a small amount of batter into each waffle cavity about halfway up. Bake for 6–8 minutes or until golden brown. Remove from the oven and let cool for 2–3 minutes before unmolding.

5. To make the whipped maple butter: In the bowl of a stand mixer fitted with a paddle attachment, add the very soft butter, maple syrup, and powdered sugar. Whip on medium speed for at least 10 minutes. Scrape down the sides of the bowl and whip for 5 minutes longer. The mixture should be extremely pale in color and very fluffy. Add the milk and whip for 5 minutes longer. Scrape into a bowl and top with the flaky sea salt. Serve right away with the warm waffle sticks.

6. Baked waffle sticks can be frozen in a zip-top bag for up to 3 weeks. Pop into the toaster oven or oven before serving or for a quick and easy breakfast.

Variations
Try making the whipped butter with honey or vanilla bean paste.

Delicate Sandwich Cookies

The texture of this cookie is similar to that of walking in freshly fallen snow: slightly crisp on the outside, with a soft, melting center. The chocolate ganache adds another depth of flavor and creamy texture that makes these so delicious. I keep these on hand in the refrigerator for any unannounced company or guest arrivals. Always a win.

Yield: 20–25 sandwich cookies

Prep Time: 20 minutes

Bake Time: 15–20 minutes (depending on size)

Chill Time: 2 hours

Difficulty: Easy

Tools: Parchment paper, ruler, rubber spatula, piping bag, round tip, silicone mat

For the Cookies

130 g (½ cup + 1 tablespoon) unsalted butter, at room temperature

160 g (1½ cups) powdered sugar

9 g (2 teaspoons) vanilla bean paste or 1 vanilla bean, split and scraped

60 g (2) egg whites, at room temperature

120 g (1 cup) all-purpose flour

30 g (¼ cup) cornstarch

30 ml (2 tablespoons) whole milk, at room temperature

1 batch Ganache 2:1 Ratio (page 54)

Chef Tips

To get the texture of the cookies just right—lightly crispy on the outside and melt-in-your-mouth smooth in the middle—use ingredients at room temperature and take your time combining the batter so it is completely smooth.

1. Preheat the oven to 325°F (160°C). Line two or three baking sheets with parchment paper and trace 3-inch (7.5-cm) vertical lines equally spaced 1 inch (2.5 cm) apart. Flip the paper upside down and use as a stencil to pipe small sticks of batter. Make sure the lines are staggered and not next to each other.

2. To make the cookies: In a mixing bowl with a spatula or in a stand mixer fitted with a paddle attachment, add the butter. This is the most important part of the recipe. The butter should be pommade consistency, like lotion, very spreadable and soft. Add the powdered sugar and vanilla paste or seeds and mix to combine. Add the egg whites one at a time, mixing in between each addition for 2–3 minutes until smooth.

3. Add the flour and cornstarch all at once. Mix on low speed for 2–3 minutes. Scrape down the sides of the bowl, add the milk, and mix for 1 minute longer. The batter should be perfectly smooth without any lumps at all. Transfer the batter to a piping bag fitted with a small round tip. If you don't have one, you can pipe these without the tip.

4. Pipe small sticks onto the prepared baking sheets following the lines. Place a sheet of parchment paper directly on top and push down gently to flatten out the batter, creating a wider shape. Freeze for 10 minutes.

5. Peel off the top parchment gently from the cookies. Bake for 15–20 minutes, rotating the baking sheet halfway through, until ONLY the edges are golden brown. Remove from the oven and let cool completely.

6. Pipe a small amount of ganache on half of the cookies and sandwich them together. Refrigerater for 2 hours to set.

7. Store an airtight container in the refrigerator for up to 5 days. Do not freeze.

Variations

Try flavoring the ganache with coffee extract or a shot (30 ml, or 1 oz) of espresso, removing 15 ml (1 tablespoon) of the heavy cream. You can also infuse the cream with mint, raspberry jam, or any other flavor variation.

Chocolate Pudding Cups
(Chocolate Pots de Crème)

These small chocolate pots de crème come together easily and are so delicious. It is very common to see these in Paris as a snack for young kids. The velvety creamy texture is decadent and just so nostalgic. You'll never eat a regular pudding cup again.

Yield: 6 small cups about 170 g (6 oz) each

Prep Time: 15 minutes

Bake Time: 15–20 minutes

Chill Time: 2 hours

Difficulty: Easy

Tools: Balloon whisk, 6 oven-safe 4-inch- (10-cm-) tall ramekins, baking dish for water bath, foil

180 g (1⅛ cups) dark chocolate chips

300 ml (1¼ cups) whole milk

300 ml (1¼ cups) heavy cream

100 g (½ cup) granulated sugar

50 g (1) egg, at room temperature

100 g (5) egg yolks, at room temperature

Chef Tips
Use eggs at room temperature to allow them to incorporate into the mixture more easily. Also avoid letting the sugar sit on the eggs without whisking the two together—this can burn the eggs and create lumps in the mixture.

1. Preheat the oven to 350°F (175°C).

2. Place the chocolate chips in a heat-safe bowl. In a 3- or 4-qt (2.7- or 3.6-l) saucepan, add the milk, heavy cream, and 50 g (¼ cup) of the sugar. Bring to a boil over medium-high heat and pour over the chocolate chips. Let stand for 20 seconds. Whisk together for 2 minutes until smooth and shiny.

3. In a large bowl, add the egg, egg yolks, and remaining 50 g (¼ cup) of sugar. Whisk for 2–3 minutes until combined. Pour the chocolate milk mixture over the eggs slowly and whisk to create a velvety smooth chocolate cream.

4. Divide the mixture among the six ramekins. Place the ramekins in a baking dish that is large enough to have room between them and a 2- or 3-inch (5- or 7.5-cm) border all around, similar to baking a cheesecake in a water bath. Add enough water to the dish to come halfway up the ramekins. Cover the dish with foil and poke two or three holes in the foil.

5. Bake for 15-20 minutes, or until the edges are fully set and the center is still slightly jiggly. Carefully remove from the oven, remove the foil, and remove the ramekins from the water bath. Set aside for 20 minutes. Chill in the refrigerator for at least 2 hours to set completely.

6. Store in the refrigerator for up to 5 days and enjoy cold. Serve plain or with a little whipped cream and berries.

Variations
Try using milk chocolate chips in the same amount but reduce the total sugar to 50 g (¼ cup).

Let's Celebrate

Many of the desserts in this section use techniques found in the Fundamentals section of this book. French baking is essentially made up of building blocks of creams, custards, cake layers, and meringues that, as you master, you can use to make into many different cakes and preparations. It is all about mastering the basics to show them off in this section. I named this section "Let's Celebrate" because these are some of my favorite recipes that are all shareable to create special moments with your friends and family. Dessert is served!

Golden Rocher Pound Cake

Is there anything better than the aroma of warm pound cake just pulled from the oven? The chocolate exterior on this cake is a technique I learned from several chefs I worked with in Paris. Every pound cake has a unique glaze, coating, or topping to preserve its delicate crumb on the inside. The shell helps keep the cake moist for days and creates a wonderful balance in textures between the fluffy cake crumb, the nutty toasted almonds, and the dark chocolate coating.

Yield: One 9 x 4-inch (23 x 10-cm) loaf cake

Prep Time: 20 minutes

Bake Time: 30–35 minutes

Chill Time: 1 hours

Difficulty: Easy

Tools: 9 x 4-inch (23 x 10-cm) loaf pan, stand mixer, rubber spatula, offset spatula

For the Pound Cake

170 g (¾ cup) unsalted butter, at room temperature

100 g (½ cup) granulated sugar

70 g (⅓ cup) light brown sugar

2 vanilla beans, split and scraped, or 9 g (2 teaspoons) vanilla bean paste

100 g (2) eggs, at room temperature

200 g (1¾ cups) all-purpose flour

10 g (2 teaspoons) baking powder

45 ml (3 tablespoons) whole milk, at room temperature

1. Preheat the oven to 350°F (175°C). Brush a large loaf pan with butter and line it with parchment paper.

2. To make the pound cake: In the bowl of a stand mixer fitted with a paddle attachment, add the butter, granulated sugar, brown sugar, and vanilla seeds or paste. Beat on medium speed for 6–8 minutes, until the mixture is very fluffy and pale in color. Scrape down the sides of the bowl and add the eggs one at time, mixing for 2 minutes in between each addition.

3. In a separate bowl, combine the flour and baking powder and mix together. Add to the butter mixture and beat for 1 minute. Scrape down the sides of the bowl, add the milk, and beat for 2 minutes longer. The batter should be completely smooth. Pour the batter into the prepared pan and place on a baking sheet on the center rack in the oven. If you have additional batter, bake the remainder in a cupcake pan.

4. Bake for 30–35 minutes, or until a knife inserted into the center comes out completely clean and the top is dark golden brown. Let cool on a wire rack for 15 minutes, then unmold the cake and let cool for 2 hours.

5. To make the rocher topping: Spread the slivered almonds on a baking sheet and bake for 5 minutes, until golden. Remove from the oven and roughly chop into small pieces.

6. Combine the chocolate and coconut oil in a microwave-safe bowl. Melt in 20-second increments, stirring in between each interval, until completely melted. Add the toasted almonds and stir to combine.

7. Place the cake on a wire rack over a baking sheet lined with plastic wrap underneath. Pour the chocolate rocher topping over the cake as evenly as you can and use an offset spatula to spread it evenly and coat the entire surface and sides of the cake. Remove from the rack with an offset spatula and place on a serving plate; chill in the refrigerator for 1 hour to set the topping.

For the Rocher Topping

75 g (½ cup) slivered almonds

220 g (1⅓ cups) dark
  chocolate chips

20 g (1½ tablespoons)
  coconut oil

8. Save any excess rocher topping by rolling the plastic wrap
into a log and squeezing to pour it back into the bowl.

9. Store the cake at room temperature for up to 5 days.

Birthday Sheet Cake

The classic vanilla sheet cake is a staple recipe we should all have in our back pockets. This one comes together so easily and has just the right amount of sweetness from the fluffy vanilla buttercream frosting. Who needs to wait for birthdays to have the corner piece of this amazing cake? The best part is you can easily turn this recipe into any flavor combination you want, but I have a sweet spot for warm buttery vanilla cake and creamy frosting.

Yield: One 9 × 13-inch (23 × 33-cm) cake

Prep Time: 20 minutes

Bake Time: 35 minutes

Chill Time: 2 hours

Difficulty: Easy

Tools: 9 × 13-inch (23 × 33-cm) cake pan, stand mixer, rubber spatula, small spoon

For the Cake

320 g (2⅔ cups) all-purpose flour

40 g (⅓ cup) cornstarch

10 g (2 teaspoons) baking powder

6 g (2 teaspoons) baking soda

180 g (1 cup) granulated sugar

150 g (3) eggs, at room temperature

20 g (1) egg yolk, at room temperature

90 g (6 tablespoons) unsalted butter, melted

30 ml (2 tablespoons) grapeseed oil

120 g (½ cup) plain full-fat yogurt, at room temperature

1 batch American Buttercream (page 46)

80 g (½ cup) sprinkles

Chef Tips

Always use butter and eggs at room temperature to get the perfect fluffy cake. Cream the butter and sugar together for several minutes until light and fluffy and doubled in volume.

1. Preheat the oven to 350°F (175°C). Brush a 9 × 13-inch (23 × 33-cm) cake pan with butter and line it with parchment paper.

2. To make the cake: In the bowl of a stand mixer fitted with a paddle attachment, add the flour, cornstarch, baking powder, baking soda, and sugar. Mix together for 1 minute to combine.

3. In a separate bowl, add the eggs, egg yolk, butter, oil, and yogurt. Be sure to use ingredients at room temperature. If your yogurt is cold, it will solidify the melted butter and create lumps in the batter. Whisk to combine.

4. Stream the yogurt mixture into the dry ingredients in the stand mixer. Mix on medium speed for 2–3 minutes until smooth. Scrape down the sides of the bowl and mix for 1 minute longer until smooth.

5. Pour the batter into the prepared pan and bake for 30–40 minutes, until golden brown, firm to the touch with a slight bounce, and a toothpick inserted into the center comes out clean. Remove from the oven and let cool completely for 1 hour.

6. Spread the buttercream across the sheet cake evenly, creating waves using the back of a small spoon, and top with the sprinkles.

7. Store the cake at room temperature for up to 4 days.

Citrus Sunset Cake with Honey Glaze

This citrus cake is a work of art and sure to dress up any dinner table. This cake uses the "tatin" method of pouring a butter caramel into the pan and having it candy the fruits onto the cake layer, creating this beautiful sunset effect. I use a combination of oranges, lemons, and blood oranges to create those colors. The key is to also make a light golden caramel to keep the fruits vibrant and bright.

Yield: One 9-inch (23-cm) cake, 8 servings

Prep Time: 20 minutes

Bake Time: 30–35 minutes

Difficulty: Easy

Tools: 9-inch (23-cm) cake pan, pastry brush, stand mixer, balloon whisk

For the Caramel and Citrus Layer

250 g (1¼ cups) granulated sugar

100 ml (½ cup) water

65 g (4 tablespoons) unsalted butter, at room temperature

1 lemon, sliced ¼ inch (6 mm) thick, with rind

1 orange, sliced ¼ inch (6 mm) thick, with rind

1 blood orange, sliced ¼ inch (6 mm) thick, with rind

For the Cake

150 g (1¼ cups) all-purpose flour

10 g (2 teaspoons) baking powder

150 g (¾ cup) granulated sugar

100 g (2) eggs, at room temperature

20 g (1) egg yolk, at room temperature

170 g (¾ cup) unsalted butter, melted

120 ml (½ cup) whole milk, at room temperature

1. Preheat the oven to 350°F (175°C).

2. To make the caramel and citrus layer: In a 3-qt (2.7-l) saucepan, add the sugar and water. Make sure all the sugar crystals are covered by the water and mix with a spatula to keep the sugar from sticking to the bottom until the mixture begins to bubble. Cook over medium heat, *without stirring*, until amber in color, 10–12 minutes. Add the butter, 1 tablespoon (14 g) at a time, and whisk to combine. Pour the caramel into a 9-inch (23-cm) cake pan and tilt the pan so the caramel coats the bottom evenly. Let set for 5 minutes, until the caramel hardens.

3. Arrange the citrus slices on the caramel, starting with the lemon on the top, orange in the middle, and blood orange on the bottom. The entire pan should be covered.

4. To make the cake: In a mixing bowl or bowl of a stand mixer fitted with the paddle attachment, add the flour, baking powder, and sugar. Mix for 1 minute to combine. In a separate bowl, add the eggs, egg yolk, melted butter, and milk. Be sure to use ingredients at room temperature. If the milk is cold it will solidify the melted butter and create lumps in the batter. Beat on medium speed for 1 minute until smooth.

5. Pour the batter into the pan over the citrus slices. Place the pan on a baking sheet on the center rack and bake for 30–35 minutes, until golden brown, firm to the touch with a slight bounce, and a toothpick inserted into the center comes out clean.

6. Remove from the oven and let cool for 10 minutes before unmolding.

7. Flip the cake over onto a plate—be careful, as there may be some juice from the citrus slices. Let cool to room temperature.

For the Glaze

50 g (2 tablespoons) light golden
  honey

Chef Tips

*See the Caramel section for tips and
tricks for making caramel. Rule #1 is
to use a very clean saucepan, and rule
#2 is never to stir the sugar once it
starts to bubble.*

8. When ready to serve, in a small microwave-safe bowl, heat
the honey for 20 seconds to liquefy. Using a pastry brush,
brush a thin layer of honey on the cake to give it a shiny finish.

9. Serve right away, or store for up to 3 days in an airtight
container at room temperature.

Basque Cake
(Gâteau Basque)

This cake is scrumptious. From the flaky, buttery crust to the creamy vanilla custard baked on the inside, it hits every mark. The custard adds a depth of flavor and texture similar to that of a giant hug! This cake gets its name from the Basque region, which sits on the border between France and northern Spain. In the Basque language, the name is *etxeko biskotxa*, or "cake of the house." It was created in the 1800s simply to celebrate that "at home feeling." So, welcome home!

Yield: One 9-inch (23-cm) cake, 8 servings

Prep Time: 30 minutes (plus master recipe)

Chill Time: 2½ hours

Bake Time: 45 minutes

Difficulty: Intermediate

Tools: Stand mixer, pastry brush, rubber spatula, 9-inch (23-cm) cake pan, rolling pin

For the Flaky Dough

120 g (½ cup + 1 tablespoon) unsalted butter, at room temperature

200 g (1 cup) granulated sugar

100 g (2) eggs, at room temperature

340 g (2¾ cups) all-purpose flour, plus more for dusting

10 g (2 teaspoons) baking powder

1 batch Pastry Cream (page 44), chilled

1. Preheat the oven to 375°F (190°C). Brush a 9-inch (23-cm) cake pan with butter and dust with flour. Line the bottom with a round of parchment paper.

2. In the bowl of a stand mixer fitted with a paddle attachment, add the butter and sugar. Cream together on medium speed for 2–3 minutes, until smooth and creamy. Add the eggs one at a time, mixing on high speed in between each addition. Scrape down the sides of the bowl and add the flour and, baking powder. Mix on medium speed for 1 minute to combine. Finish combining the dough by hand to avoid overmixing and shape it into a thick disk (pancake shape).

3. Divide the dough into two-thirds and one-third. The two-thirds will make up the base and sides of the cake, and the one-third will make up the top.

4. Press two-thirds of the dough along the bottom and sides of the prepared pan on top of the parchment paper as neatly and evenly as you can. You can use the bottom of a measuring cup to flatten out the dough so that its nice and even. Wrap the remaining one-third of dough in plastic wrap and set aside at room temperature. Place the pan in the refrigerator for 30 minutes to chill the base of the cake.

5. Pour the chilled pastry cream into the chilled crust. Spread it out evenly. On a lightly floured surface, roll out the reserved dough. Cut a ring the size of the pan and place it on top of the pastry cream.

6. Make the egg wash: In a small bowl, whisk together the eggs, egg yolk, heavy cream, and sugar. Brush the egg wash over the dough evenly and lightly. Score with a fork into crisscross patterns however you like for a fun design and brush with egg wash once more.

For the Egg Wash

100 g (2) eggs, at room temperature

20 g (1) egg yolk, at room temperature

20 ml (4 teaspoons) heavy cream

5 g (1¼ teaspoon) granulated sugar

Powdered sugar, for dusting (optional)

7. Bake for 20 minutes. Reduce the oven temperature to 350°F (175°C) and bake for 20 minutes longer. Rotate the pan and bake 5 minutes longer, until dark golden brown.

8. Remove from the oven and let cool in the pan for 20–30 minutes. Then flip the cake over onto a plate, remove the parchment paper on the bottom, and flip it right-side up. Chill for 2 hours in the refrigerator and serve cold. If desired, dust with powdered sugar before serving.

9. Store in an airtight container in the refrigerator for up to 4 days. Do not freeze.

Variations

Add 100 g (3½ oz) of melted dark chocolate to the pastry cream to make a chocolate version. Add 20 g (¾ oz) of cocoa powder to the dough as well.

'90s Brownies

These iconic brownies made their first debut in September 1999. Today, French pastry chef meets these nostalgic '90s brownies to re-create an even fudgier, more delicious gourmet version. This brownie has all the rich, dense chocolaty goodness with an elevated creamy chocolate ganache, topped with colorful chips for all the lunchbox memory feels.

Yield: 18 brownies

Prep Time: 20 minutes

Bake Time: 30–40 minutes

Chill Time: 1 hour

Difficulty: Easy

Tools: 9 x 13-inch (23 x 33-cm) cake pan, stand mixer, rubber spatula, offset spatula

For the Brownies

170 g (¾ cup) unsalted butter, at room temperature

26 g (2 tablespoons) grapeseed oil or neutral oil

250 g (1¼ cups) granulated sugar

200 g (1 cup) light brown sugar

200 g (4) eggs, at room temperature

250 g (2⅛ cups) all-purpose flour

10 g (2 teaspoons) baking powder

40 g (⅓ cup) cocoa powder

For Decorating

1 batch Ganache 2:1 Ratio (page 54)

80 g (⅓ cup) colored candy chocolate chips

Chef Tips

Using a high-quality chocolate in this recipe is important, as it is the most important ingredient to obtain a rich, chewy, brownie texture. Make sure the eggs and butter are at room temperature to obtain the right batter consistency. The butter should be soft and completely spreadable.

1. Preheat the oven to 350°F (175°C). Brush a 9 x 13-inch (23 x 33-cm) baking pan with butter and line it with parchment paper and set aside.

2. To make the brownies: In a stand mixer fitted with a paddle attachment or in a bowl using a spatula, add the butter, oil, granulated sugar, and brown sugar. Cream together on medium speed for 3–4 minutes. Stop the mixer to scrape down the sides of the bowl a few times. Once the mixture is nice and fluffy, add the eggs one at a time as you continuing mixing.

3. Add the flour, baking powder, and cocoa powder. Mix on low speed for 2 minutes, then stream in the milk. Scrape down the sides of the bowl one last time and mix for 1 minute longer, until smooth.

4. Pour the batter into the prepared pan and spread it evenly using an offset spatula.

5. Bake for 30–40 minutes, until a toothpick inserted into the center comes out clean. Remove from the oven and set aside to cool in the pan for several minutes.

6. To finish the brownies: Pour the chocolate ganache all over the brownies, spreading it evenly with an offset spatula. Let set for 5 minutes. Top with the colorful chocolate chips for decoration.

7. Chill in the refrigerator for 1 hour for the ganache to set.

8. Store at room temperature for up to 4 days or freeze, wrapped in plastic wrap, for up to 3 weeks.

Pillowy Soft Cinnamon Sugar Pretzels

Brunch will never be the same once you've added these to the menu. They will be a fan favorite and on constant repeat. These pretzels are pillowy soft with a crispier bite on the outside and dunked in butter and cinnamon sugar. The best part is you don't need to spend hours in the kitchen, because they come together in under 2 hours from the oven to the table.

Yield 6 large pretzels

Prep Time 20 minutes

Bake Time 15–20 minutes

Rest Time 20 minutes

Difficulty Easy

Tools Silicone mat, stand mixer, pastry brush, large pot

For the Pretzels

235 ml (1 cup) whole milk

7 g (2¼ teaspoons or 1 packet) active dry yeast

20 g (1½ tablespoons) light brown sugar

480 g (4 cups) all-purpose flour

80 g (⅓ cup) granulated sugar

30 g (2 tablespoons) unsalted butter, melted

For the Baking Soda Bath

2 l (8½ cups) water

130 g (½ cup) baking soda

For the Cinnamon Sugar Topping

113 g (½ cup) unsalted butter

100 g (½ cup) granulated sugar

8 g (1 tablespoon) ground cinnamon

1. Preheat the oven to 375°F (190°C). Line a baking sheet with a silicone mat or parchment paper.

2. To make the pretzels: In a 2-qt (1.8-l) saucepan, warm the milk over low heat until lukewarm but not hot. Set aside.

3. In a small bowl, add the yeast, brown sugar, and ¼ cup (60 ml) of the warm milk. Mix together and set aside for 10 minutes to autolyze the yeast (page 25), making sure it's active and ready to use.

4. In the bowl of a stand mixer fitted with a hook attachment, add the flour and granulated sugar. Mix together for a few seconds just to combine. Once the yeast mixture is frothy, stream it into the dry ingredients as you mix on low speed. Stream in the remaining 180 ml (¾ cup) of warm milk. Add the melted butter and continue kneading for 15–20 minutes. The dough should be smooth and shiny. Perform the windowpane test (page 25) to ensure the dough is kneaded sufficiently so the pretzels will be fluffy.

5. Oil a large bowl. Roll the dough into a ball, place it in the bowl, turn to coat, and cover with a clean dish towel for 20 minutes to bench proof. It will grow 1½ times in size.

6. Press down on the dough to releases the gas and place the dough on your work surface. No need to flour the work surface. This is not a sticky dough. Divide the dough evenly into six balls. Roll each one into a log, form into a "U" shape, and cross the ends of the log at the top. Push back down into the center, creating a pretzel shape. Place each pretzel on the prepared baking sheet and set aside.

7. To make the baking soda bath: Fill a large pot with the water and baking soda and bring to a boil over high heat. Dunk each pretzel, one at a time, in the bath for 20 seconds. The longer you leave the pretzels, the darker and more "bitter pretzel" flavor you will create. Do not go past 30 seconds. Place each pretzel back on the baking sheet.

8. Bake for 15–20 minutes, until completely golden brown on the top and bottom. Remove from the oven and transfer the pretzels, to a cooling rack. Let them cool for 20–30 minutes.

9. To make the cinnamon sugar topping: In a microwave-safe bowl, melt the butter. In a large bowl, add the sugar and cinnamon and whisk to combine. Brush or dunk each pretzel one at time in the butter and then roll in the cinnamon sugar to coat. Serve right away or store for up 2 days in an airtight container.

Variations

Remove the sugar and sugar topping from the recipe and try a savory version with the same amount of grated Parmesan.

Paris-Brest to Share
(Paris-Brest à Partager)

As the story goes, this famous French pastry was first created to honor a bicycle race that took place every year in Paris-Brest. The organizer, Pierre Giffard, asked local pastry chef Louis Durand to create a dessert. Its circular form honors the wheel shape of the bicycle, and the cake, choux puffs filled with hazelnut praline pastry cream whipped with butter into a super creamy mousseline filling, is rich and decadent. It is irresistible and a labor of true love.

Yield: 6–8 servings

Prep Time: 1 hour (plus master recipes)

Bake Time: 35–45 minutes

Chill Time: 1 hour

Difficulty: Intermediate

Tools: Silicone mat, piping bag with round and star tips, balloon whisk, pastry brush, stand mixer, serrated knife, offset spatula

1 batch Pâte à Choux Dough (page 38)

22 g (2 ⅓ tablespoons) chopped hazelnuts

For the Egg Wash

100 g (2) eggs, at room temperature

20 g (1) egg yolk, at room temperature

20 ml (4 teaspoons) heavy cream

5 g (1¼ teaspoons) granulated sugar

For the Mousseline

1 batch Pastry Cream (page 44), chilled

113 g (½ cup) unsalted butter, at room temperature

65 g (3½ tablespoons) Hazelnut Praline Paste (page 53)

Powdered sugar, for dusting

1. Preheat the oven to 350°F (175°C). Line a baking sheet with a silicone mat or parchment paper. Fit a piping bag with a round tip and another with a star tip and set aside.

2. Transfer the pâte à choux dough to the piping bag with the round tip. Pipe an 8-inch (20-cm) circle on the prepared baking sheet. Pipe a second circle around the outside of the first, making sure they touch. Pipe a third circle on top of both of those in the center, overlapping the other two.

3. Make the egg wash: In a small bowl, whisk together the eggs, egg yolk, heavy cream, and sugar. Brush the dough with the egg wash. Sprinkle the chopped hazelnuts over the top.

4. Bake for 35 minutes, until puffed and dark golden brown. Remove from the oven and let cool to room temperature.

5. To make the mousseline: In the bowl of a stand mixer fitted with a paddle attachment, add the chilled pastry cream. Beat on medium speed to loosen the cream. Add the butter, 15 g (1 tablespoon) at a time, and beat until the mixture is thick and fluffy. Add the praline paste and whip for 2 minutes longer, until smooth and combined. Transfer the mousseline to the piping bag with the star tip.

6. Cut the choux circle in half horizontally using a serrated knife. Set the top half to the side. Place the bottom half on a serving plate, as you won't be able to move it later on. Pipe the mousseline in a clockwise spiral motion. Take your time to make the dessert look nice. You can also pipe straight up into tall rosettes for an easier option.

7. Dust the top half with powdered sugar. Using an offset spatula, place the top gently back onto the bottom half over the cream, making sure it's centered. Refrigerate for 1 hour, and then serve right away.

8. Store the cake in an airtight container in the refrigerator for up to 2 days.

Swiss Roll *(Gâteau Roulé)*

Swiss roll is an extremely fluffy, light, and reliable roll cake. This is a wonderful cake to master and can be paired with an endless amounts of creams, custards, and fillings. This one is paired with a vanilla whipped cream and fresh berries for a light dessert at the end of a heavy meal. This cake is wonderful to use for bûche de Noël. The cornstarch is a star ingredient in the recipe, creating just the right texture and making the roll pliable and soft. A quick and easy elegant dessert—what could be better?

Yield: One 13-inch (33-cm) log, 6 servings

Prep Time: 35 minutes

Bake Time: 20 minutes

Chill Time: 2–3 hours

Difficulty: Intermediate

Tools: Silicone mat, stand mixer, rubber spatula, offset spatula, piping bag, paring knife, St. Honoré piping tip

For the Cake

120 g (6) egg yolks, at room temperature

110 g (½ cup + 2 tablespoons) granulated sugar, divided

150 g (5) egg whites, at room temperature

60 ml (¼ cup) whole milk

60 ml (¼ cup) grapeseed oil or neutral oil

9 g (2 teaspoons) vanilla bean paste

45 g (⅓ cup) all-purpose flour

41 g (⅓ cup) cornstarch

For the Whipped Cream and Toppings

300 ml (1¼ cups) heavy cream

100 g (1 cup) powdered sugar

4 g (1 teaspoon) vanilla bean paste or 1 vanilla bean, split and scraped

170 g (1 cup) fresh raspberries

100 g (⅔ cup) fresh blueberries

75 g (½ cup) fresh blackberries

1. Preheat the oven to 325°F (160°C). Line a baking sheet with a silicone mat or parchment paper.

2. To make the cake: In the bowl of a stand mixer fitted with a whisk attachment, add the egg yolks and 2 tablespoons (30 g) of the granulated sugar. Whisk for 10 minutes on high speed until thickened, pale in color, and doubled in volume. Gently pour the egg mixture into a large mixing bowl and set aside.

3. Quickly wash and dry the stand mixer bowl VERY well, as the tiniest amount of fat left over from the yolks can prevent the meringue from rising. Add the egg whites and remaining ½ cup (90 g) of granulated sugar. Whisk on high speed until stiff peaks form, 8–10 minutes.

4. Meanwhile, in a small bowl, add the milk, oil, and vanilla paste or seeds. Whisk to combine and set aside.

5. In a separate bowl, add the flour and cornstarch. Mix to combine and set aside. Now you should have four different preparations to combine. The egg yolk mixture, the meringue, the dry ingredients, and the wet ingredients.

6. Add the yolk mixture to the egg whites and gently fold with a rubber spatula by hand. Alternate adding the flour mixture and the milk mixture until everything is fully incorporated. Be careful not to deflate the eggs or the cake will be very thin.

7. Pour the batter onto the prepared baking sheet and spread it out evenly with an offset spatula. Bake for 20 minutes, until completely golden brown and slightly bouncy to the touch. Remove from the oven, slide the mat off the baking sheet, and let cool to room temperature.

8. To make the whipped cream: In the bowl of a stand mixer fitted with a whisk attachment, add the heavy cream, powdered sugar, and vanilla. Whisk until stiff peaks form, 2–3 minutes.

9. Using a small paring knife, detach the cake layer from the edges of the baking sheet. Set up your workstation with the whipped cream, a piping bag fitted with a St. Honoré piping tip, the cake, the berries, and an offset spatula. Spread one-third of the whipped cream evenly on the cake. Place some berries all over the cream, alternating the raspberries, blueberries, and blackberries.

10. Begin to roll up the cake tightly, peeling off the parchment paper or silicone mat as you go. Try to roll it as tightly as possible so that perfect escargot (snail) shape will be revealed in every slice.

11. Spread another one-third of the whipped cream all over the top of the cake. Transfer the rest of the whipped cream to the piping bag. Pipe the whipped cream across the top of the cake, going from left to right in a constant motion to create beautiful waves. Place a few more berries across the top.

12. Chill the cake in the refrigerator for 2–3 hours, until completely set. Serve cold, and store any leftover cake in the refrigerator for up to 3 days.

Variations

Fold 50 g (1¾ oz) of melted dark chocolate into the whipped cream for a chocolate version. Feel free to also use strawberries or peaches for a great alternative. For a final touch, add just a little bit of edible gold dust for an elegant look.

Soft as Cotton Cheesecake
(Japanese-Inspired Cheesecake)

I have never been a fan of the classic cheesecake, as I have always found it a little bit too dense and not delicate enough in flavor and texture. When I discovered the Japanese cheesecake several years ago, I made it my mission to create a recipe that would be reliable and easy to make. The texture is unlike anything else. Cheesecake meets soufflé in this incredible light and airy dessert. It has all the wonderful flavors of classic cheesecake without any of the dense consistency. It is like a eating a cloud flavored with cheesecake. It takes a little practice to get this one just right, but it is so worth the effort.

Yield: One 6-inch (15-cm) cheesecake, 6 servings

Prep Time: 25 minutes

Bake Time: 1 hour

Difficulty: Intermediate

Tools: 6 x 4-inch (15 x 10-cm) cake pan, stand mixer, rubber spatula, bain-marie

For the Cake

65 g (4 tablespoons) unsalted butter

225 g (8 oz) cream cheese

120 ml (½ cup) whole milk

80 g (4) egg yolks, at room temperature

100 g (½ cup) granulated sugar, divided

20 g (2 tablespoons) cornstarch

40 g (⅓ cup) all-purpose flour

120 g (4) egg whites, at room temperature

For the Fruit Topping

170 g (1 cup) fresh raspberries

100 g (⅔ cup) fresh blueberries

75 g (½ cup) fresh blackberries

30 g (¼ cup) powdered sugar

1. Preheat the oven to 330°F (165°C). Brush a 6 x 4-inch (15 x 10-cm) cake pan with butter and line it with parchment paper along the bottom and sides.

2. To make the cake: In a 3-qt (2.7-l) saucepan, add the butter, cream cheese, and milk. Heat over low heat, stirring, until melted and completely smooth. There should be no lumps at all. Remove from the heat and set aside for a few minutes until warm, but not hot.

3. Add the egg yolks, 50 g (¼ cup) of the granulated sugar, cornstarch, and flour. Whisk until completely smooth.

4. In the mixing bowl of a stand mixer fitted with a whisk attachment, add the egg whites and remaining 50 g (¼ cup) of granulated sugar. Whisk on medium speed until stiff peaks form, about 8 minutes.

5. Gently take one-third of the meringue and whisk it by hand into the egg yolk mixture. Then pour that mixture back into the rest of the meringue and fold together very gently using a spatula. Take your time, as this is the most important part of the recipe. Pour the batter right away into the prepared cake pan.

6. Set up a bain-marie (water bath): Place the cake pan in the center of a large baking pan and fill the large pan halfway with water. Carefully transfer to the oven. Bake for 20 minutes. This is when the cake will rise. DO NOT OPEN the oven. Once the cake is nice and tall, reduce the oven temperature to 250°F (120°C) and bake for 40 minutes longer. Keep an eye on the cake to make sure it is not cracking on top. If you see it start to crack, reduce the oven temperature to 230°F (110°C) and bake for 10 minutes longer, or until a knife inserted into the center comes out completely clean. Keep an eye on the water level, making sure it stays about halfway up the sides as the cheesecake is baking.

7. Remove from the oven and set on a cooling rack for 30 minutes before unmolding.

8. To make the fruit topping: Decorate the cake with the berries and dust with powdered sugar. Serve immediately. Do not refrigerate this cake, as the texture will become dense and heavy. Do not freeze. Enjoy within 1–2 days.

Variations

Try adding lemon or orange zest. For a chocolate version, add 20 g (¾ oz) of cocoa powder and reduce the flour by 20 g (¾ oz).

Mille Crêpes Cake

Dutch *poffertjes*, Indian *dosas*, Russian *blini*, Japanese *hirayachi*, French crepes:
Every culture has its own version of the "pan cake." Get it? The mille crepes cake is a fun
dessert with alternating layers of crepes and vanilla whipped cream. Translated in French
it means "a thousand crepes," but this one has fifteen crepes, and because we need to
make it beautiful, the top is torched with a sweet sugar crust for a crunchy bite.

Yield: One 9-inch (23-cm) cake,
8 servings

Prep Time: 20 minutes
(plus master recipe)

Chill Time: 4 hours

Difficulty: Easy

Tools: Stand mixer, offset spatula,
kitchen torch

For the Whipped Cream Filling

240 ml (1 cup) heavy cream

110 g (1 cup) powdered sugar

4 g (1 teaspoon) vanilla bean paste

For the Cake

1 batch Pretty Buttery Crepes
(page 55), cooked and chilled

100 g (½ cup) granulated sugar

Chef Tips

*Make the crepes ahead of time
so they have time to chill and you
aren't waiting on them to assemble
the cake. You can freeze the
assembled cake for up to 1 month
without the sugar topping.*

1. To make the whipped cream filling: In the bowl of a stand
mixer fitted with a whisk attachment, add the heavy cream,
powdered sugar, and vanilla. Whisk on medium speed until
stiff peaks form, 2–3 minutes; do not overwhip or the cream
filling will get grainy. Set aside.

2. To assemble the cake: Place one crepe on a serving plate.
Using an offset spatula, spread a thin layer of whipped cream,
stack another crepe on top, and repeat the process until you
have used all the crepes. Use the remaining whipped cream
to cover the top and outside of the cake with a thin layer.
Refrigerate the cake for 4 hours.

3. When ready to serve, pour the granulated sugar on top and
torch with a kitchen torch. Serve immediately. Store this cake
in the refrigerator for up to 5 days. This dessert gets better
over the days as the vanilla flavors develop in the crepes and
whipped cream together.

Variations

You can add 8 g (4 teaspoons) of cocoa powder to the whipped cream for a
chocolate version. You can also switch up the filling and add jam or chocolate
spread. The important part is to always refrigerate this cake before cutting so it
holds its elegant shape and displays all the layers.

Tropézienne Tart
(Brioche Cake)

Tropézienne tart, or tart from St. Tropez, was first created by pastry chef Alexandre Micka. He owned a patisserie in St. Tropez and wanted to bring his Polish grandmother's traditional cake to France. But it was not until Brigitte Bardot, who was shooting a film in St. Tropez, "discovered" the tart that word of it spread. The tart has since become very popular all over France. The first version was a sliced brioche filled with lemon curd and pastry cream, topped with pearl sugar. My version is little bit lighter and uses a crème légère, bringing creaminess from the baked custard and a nice airy texture from the whipped cream. It's just as delicious as the original.

Yield: One 10-inch (25-cm) cake

Prep Time: 30 minutes (plus master recipes)

Rest Time: 3 hours

Bake Time: 30–35 minutes

Chill Time: 1 hour

Difficulty: Intermediate

Tools: 10-inch (25-cm) tart ring pan, rubber spatula, piping bag, round tip or star tip, pastry brush, serrated knife

1 batch French Brioche Dough (page 35), unbaked

For the Egg Wash

Use the same as Basque cake

100 g (½ cup) pearl sugar crystals

1 batch Crème Légère (page 45)

Powdered sugar, for dusting

1. Place the brioche dough in a 10-inch (25-cm) tart ring pan. Flatten it out and dock small holes in the top with a fork. This will allow for a more even proof and prevent any bubbles that would deform the brioche when baked. Allow to proof for 2 hours, until doubled in size. Place somewhere slightly warm and dark for faster results.

2. Brush with the egg wash and proof for 30 minutes longer.

3. When ready to bake, preheat the oven to 350°F (175°C). Brush the brioche with one more coat of egg wash and top with lots of pearl sugar. Much of it will fall off during baking.

4. Bake for 30–35 minutes, or until the top is completely dark golden brown. Remove from the oven and set on a wire rack to cool completely.

5. Transfer the crème légère to a piping bag fitted with a round piping tip or a star tip for an elegant effect. With a serrated knife, cut the brioche horizontally all the way through. Set the top off to the side and pipe large dollops of the cream all along the border and on the inside.

6. Dust the brioche top with powdered sugar and gently place it onto the cream. Chill for 30 minutes and then serve immediately.

7. Store in an airtight container in the refrigerator for up to 3 days.

Chocolate Party Pavlova

This decadent, yet light and crispy pavlova is sure to satisfy any true chocolate lover's craving. The whipped cream and chocolate ganache pair beautifully to create a light yet rich texture. The crispy chocolate meringue offers just the right amount of sweetness. This dessert comes together quickly with just a few simple ingredients and can be assembled right before serving if needed.

Yield: 6 servings

Prep Time: 25 minutes

Bake Time: 55 minutes

Chill Time: 1 hour

Difficulty: Easy

Tools: Silicone mat, stand mixer, rubber spatula, candy thermometer, piping bag, round tip, offset spatula

For the Pavlova Layers

120 g (4) egg whites, at room temperature

240 g (1¼ cups) granulated sugar

100 ml (½ cup) water

80 g (½ cup) dark chocolate chips

For the Whipped Cream

235 ml (1 cup) heavy cream

50 g (½ cup) powdered sugar

For the Chocolate Ganache

200 g (1¼ cups) dark chocolate chips

60 ml (¼ cup) heavy cream

For the Toppings

50 g (⅓ cup) mini chocolate chips

50 g (⅓ cup) chopped hazelnuts (optional)

1. Preheat the oven to 300°F (150°C). Line a baking sheet with a silicone mat or parchment paper.

2. To make the pavlova layers: In the bowl of a stand mixer fitted with a whisk attachment, add the egg whites and begin whipping on low speed to get them frothy. Simultaneously, set up a 2-qt (1.8-l) saucepan with the granulated sugar and water. Use a spatula to move around the sugar to make sure it is completely coated in water and will not stick to the bottom of the pan. Cook over medium heat, *without stirring*, until the mixture reaches 250°F (120°C) on a candy thermometer. Stream the sugar syrup into the whipping egg whites and continue whipping for 10–12 minutes. The mixing bowl should be cool to the touch and the meringue should be shiny and hold stiff peaks in the center of the bowl.

3. In a microwave-safe bowl, add the dark chocolate chips. Melt in increments of 20 seconds at a time, stirring in between each interval, until completely melted. The chocolate should be melted but not warm. If it's a little warm, allow it to cool. Fold the chocolate gently into the meringue, creating streaks and pockets of chocolate.

4. Transfer the meringue to a piping bag fitted with a round piping tip or no tip. Pipe large spiral-shaped circles as thick or as wide as you want the pavlova to be onto the prepared baking sheet. The thicker ones tend to be more fragile and take longer to bake. Make two or three layers total.

5. Transfer to the oven and bake for 25 minutes. Reduce the oven temperature to 250°F (120°C) and bake for 30 minutes longer. The meringues should be hard to the touch and completely dry. Make sure before removing them from the oven. They will be fragile. Allow them to cool completely before handling.

6. To make the whipped cream: In the bowl of a stand mixer fitted with a whisk attachment, add the heavy cream and powdered sugar. Whisk until stiff peaks form, 3–4 minutes. Set aside.

7. To make the chocolate ganache: In a microwave-safe bowl, add the dark chocolate chips and heavy cream. Melt for 30 seconds, and then let sit for 10 seconds. Whisk until smooth and shiny.

8. Set up the workstation with the meringues, the whipped cream, a cake stand, the chocolate ganache, toppings, and rubber and offset spatulas. Pipe a small amount of whipped cream on the cake stand and place the first meringue on it (this will be the glue). Pour a third of the ganache and spread it out evenly with an offset spatula, then top with some whipped cream, some mini chocolate chips, and some chopped hazelnuts. Repeat the process until you have used up all of the ingredients.

9. Refrigerate for 1 hour and serve nice and cold.

10. Store in the refrigerator for 1–2 days. The humidity from the cream will soften the meringue quickly, so if making this ahead of time, assemble 2–4 hours before for the best texture.

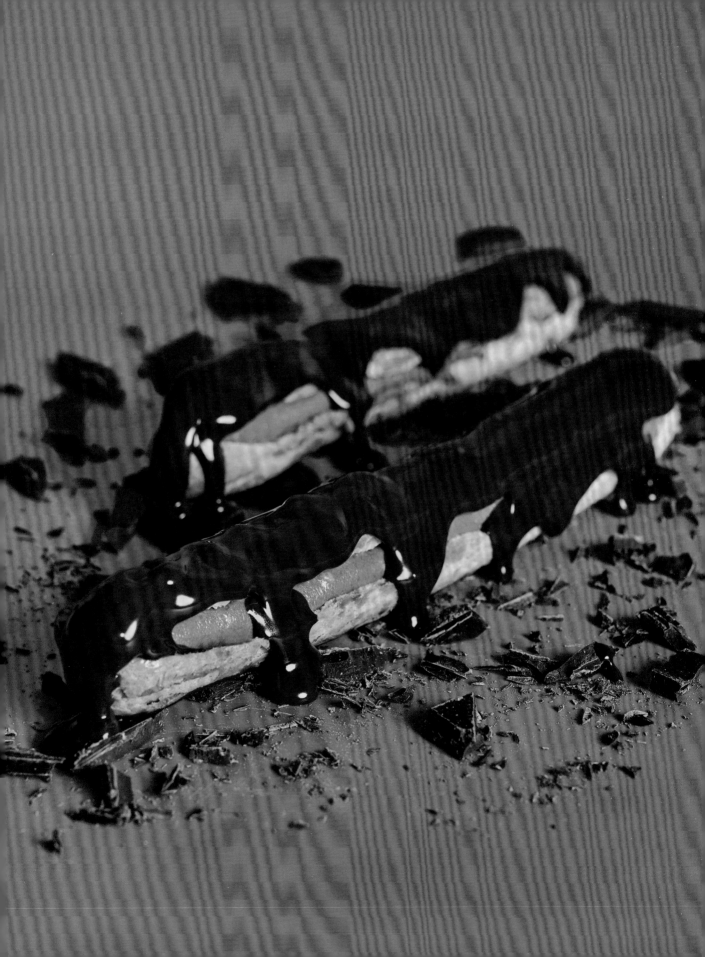

Elegant Chocolate Éclairs
(Éclairs au Chocolat)

Chef Antonin Carême holds title for making one of the first chocolate éclairs in Lyon, France, in the early 1800s. This beautiful dessert used to be called pain à la duchesse, or duchess bread. It's new name, éclair, was inspired by how quickly this delicious dessert is consumed—in a flash. It is common to spot the classic French pastry in almost every patisserie in France. It is often flavored with coffee, berries, or lemon curd for a fresh alternative. I'm a lover of this classic creamy chocolate edition with chocolate glaze.

Yield: 3–4 éclairs 10–12 inches (25–30 cm) long

Prep Time: 30 minutes (plus master recipes)

Bake Time: 22 minutes

Chill Time: 1 hour

Difficulty: Intermediate

Tools: Silicone mat, piping bag, round tip, balloon whisk, serrated knife, pastry brush, offset spatula

½ batch Pâte à Choux Dough (page 38)

For the Quick Egg Wash

50 g (1) egg

20 ml (4 teaspoons) heavy cream or whole milk

For the Chocolate Ganache Icing

200 g (1¼ cups) dark chocolate chips

45 ml (3 tablespoons) heavy cream

20 g (1½ tablespoons) coconut oil

1 batch Chocolate Pastry Cream (page 44), chilled

Chef Tips

Pipe the pâte à choux as evenly as possible. Trace a line with a pen 10–12 inches (25–30 cm) long on the parchment paper. Flip the paper over and pipe on the other side, using the lines as a stencil.

1. Preheat the oven to 350°F (175°C). Line a baking sheet with a silicone mat or parchment paper. Fit a piping bag with a round tip or no tip if you don't have one.

2. Transfer the pâte à choux dough to the prepared piping bag. On the prepared baking sheet, pipe 10- or 12-inch (25- or 30-cm) lines of dough. You can make three or four, depending on how long you pipe them.

3. To make the egg wash: In a small bowl, add the egg and heavy cream. Whisk together and gently brush onto each line of dough.

4. Bake for 20–22 minutes, until puffed and golden brown. Remove from the oven and let cool to room temperature.

5. To make the chocolate ganache: In a microwave-safe bowl, add the dark chocolate chips, heavy cream, and coconut oil. Melt for 30 seconds, and then let sit for 10 seconds. Whisk until smooth and shiny.

6. Slice each éclair in half horizontally using a serrated knife. Set the tops of each éclair off to the side. In a small bowl, add the chilled pastry cream and whisk with a balloon whisk to loosen it. Transfer the pastry cream to a piping bag and pipe all along the éclair for each one.

7. Use a pastry brush to brush a thick layer of the chocolate ganache topping onto the hats (tops) of each éclair. Carefully place the tops back onto each pastry using an offset spatula. Place the éclairs carefully on a serving tray or plate and refrigerate for 1 hour. Serve right away, or store for up to 2 days.

8. Baked, unfilled éclairs can be stored in an airtight container in the freezer for up to 3 months.

Smores Cookie Pizza

A thick and chewy chocolate chip cookie crust, creamy chocolate ganache, and warm toasty marshmallows—campfire night and camping memories have been upgraded with this gourmet beauty. It's the ultimate combo and an absolute crowd-pleaser.

Yield: One 9-inch (23-cm) cookie pizza, 8 servings

Prep Time: 30 minutes

Bake Time: 25 minutes

Difficulty: Easy

Tools: 9-inch (23–cm) baking pan, silicone mat, stand mixer, rubber spatula, offset spatula

---

113 g (½ cup) unsalted butter, at room temperature

60 g (⅓ cup) granulated sugar

100 g (½ cup) light brown sugar

50 g (1) egg, at room temperature

130 g (1⅛ cups) all-purpose flour

10 g (2 teaspoons) baking powder

100 g (¾ cup) dark chocolate chips

For Decorating

1 batch Ganache 2:1 Ratio (page 54)

284 g (10 oz) regular size marshmallows

> ### Chef Tips
> *To cook this outdoors, use a cast-iron pan on the grill and adjust the cooking time accordingly.*

1. Preheat the oven to 350°F (175°C). Brush a 9-inch (23-cm) baking pan with butter and line the bottom with parchment paper. Line a baking sheet with a silicone mat or parchment paper.

2. In the bowl of a stand mixer fitted with a paddle attachment, add the butter, granulated sugar, and brown sugar. Cream together on medium speed for 2–3 minutes. Stop twice to scrape down the sides of the bowl. The mixture should be light and creamy.

3. Add the egg mixture and mix for 2 minutes longer, until smooth. Add the flour, baking powder, and chocolate chips and mix on low speed for 1 minute, until combined.

4. Place the dough in the center of the prepared pan and spread it out evenly with an offset spatula. Bake for 25–30 minutes, until dark golden brown. Turn the oven to low broil.

5. Remove from the oven and let cool for 20 minutes. Run a knife along the edge of the pan and flip the cookie over. Peel off the parchment paper round and flip right-side up.

6. Place the cookie on the prepared baking sheet. Top the warm cookie with the chocolate ganache. Spread it out evenly using an offset spatula. Top with the marshmallows.

7. Toast the pizza under the broiler for 2 minutes. KEEP AN EYE ON IT. It can burn very quickly.

8. Store the pizza in an airtight container at room temperature for up 1 week. For optimal texture, microwave or heat up slices for 20 seconds before serving.

French Strawberry Shortcake *(Le Fraisier)*

One of the first versions of this cake was called "the bagatelle," and it was created by Gaston Lenôtre in the 1960s. The key elements are the mousseline, fresh strawberries, genoise, and marzipan. This cake is one of my personal favorites; the rich vanilla cream pairs perfectly with the fresh strawberries and there is just enough sweetness from the marzipan to tie it all together.

Yield: One 9-inch (23-cm) cake, 8 servings

Prep Time: 30 minutes (plus master recipes)

Chill Time: 30 minutes

Difficulty: Intermediate

Tools: Piping bag, round tip, 9-inch (20-cm) cake ring, cutting board, offset spatula, paring knife, kitchen torch

For the Cake

1 batch Crème Mousseline (page 45)

1 batch Genoise (page 30)

For Finishing

473 g (1 lb) fresh strawberries

200 g (¾ cup) Marzipan (page 51)

1. Load the crème mousseline into a piping bag with a round tip or no tip if you don't have one. Prepare a workstation with the genoise, crème mousseline piping bag, strawberries, marzipan, a 9-inch (20-cm) cake ring, a cutting board, an offset spatula, and a paring knife.

2. Cut half of the strawberries in half. Place the tallest ones open side against the ring around the outside of the cake.

3. Cut the genoise in half horizontally. Place one half in the center of the strawberries. Pipe crème mousseline in between each strawberry and covering the cake layer. Use an offset spatula to spread it around evenly. Chop 8 strawberries into small pieces and lay them on the cream in the center of the cake.

4. Top with a little more cream. Place the second half of the genoise on the top inside the ring so it fits right on top of the strawberries. Press down firmly to make sure everything is nice and secure.

5. Roll out the marzipan into a circle about ¼ inch (6 mm) thick and place it on top of the genoise. Freeze for 30 minutes.

6. Place the cake in the frozen ring on a cake stand and lightly torch the ring to loosen it and slide it off.

7. Decorate the top with a few more strawberry halves on top and serve cold.

8. Store in the refrigerator for up to 2 days.

Raspberry Charlotte

The Charlotte has come a long way from its early days of stacked brioches and applesauce that were baked for several hours. Named for the eighteenth-century English queen Sophie-Charlotte de Mecklembourg-Strelitz, this dessert, consisting of mousse (fruit or chocolate) and ladyfinger cake layers on the inside and a "cartouche" ring of ladyfingers along the exterior, this dessert was created by one of the most famous chefs of the time, Antonin Careme. He was also credited with creating the first version of ladyfingers as a biscuit that could be dipped in wine without falling apart.

Yield: 8 servings

Prep Time: 30 minutes (plus master recipe)

Bake Time: 25–25 minutes

Chill Time: 14 hours

Difficulty: Intermediate

Tools: Stand mixer, rubber spatula, 8-inch (20-cm) cake ring or springform pan, paring knife, offset spatula, pastry brush

For the Raspberry Mousse

14 g (7) gold gelatin sheets or 4 g (1½ tablespoons) gelatin powder

480 g (2 cups) raspberry puree

400 ml (1⅔ cups) heavy cream

140 g (⅔ cup) mascarpone

100 g (½ cup) granulated sugar

12–14 Homemade Ladyfingers + 2 disks (page 59)

For Decorating

500 g (3 cups) fresh raspberries

1 m (40 inches) ribbon (optional)

40 g (2 tablespoons) raspberry jam (optional, for shine)

Chef Tips

Use the freezer to quickly chill the charlotte as you work to build the layers so the mousse stays cold and thick.

1. To make the raspberry mousse: If using sheet gelatin, soak the sheets in a bowl of cold water for 10 minutes, until bloomed and softened. If using powder gelatin, combine the powder with 2 tablespoon of warm water and let bloom for 5 minutes. In a 3-qt (2.7-l) saucepan, add one-third of the raspberry puree. Bring to a low simmer over low heat. Add the bloomed gelatin sheets or powder, stir to combine, then add the rest of the raspberry puree. Pour the mixture onto a baking sheet and spread it out with an offset spatula. Refrigerate for 20 minutes so it cools quickly.

2. In the bowl of a stand mixer fitted with a paddle attachment, add the heavy cream, mascarpone, and sugar. Whip on medium speed until stiff peaks form, 5 minutes. Transfer to a bowl and place in the refrigerator for 15 minutes.

3. Once both the fruit puree and the whipped cream are nice and cold, fold them together gently without deflating the whipped cream. Be gentle and take your time to keep the mousse nice and thick. Place in the refrigerator for 15 minutes.

4. Prepare a workstation with an 8-inch (20-cm) cake ring or springform pan, the raspberry mousse, the ladyfingers, and the fresh raspberries. Place the ladyfingers against the ring around the outside of the cake; they should fit tightly together and all the way around. Cut one of the ladyfinger disks so it fits nice and snug in the center of the cake ring on the inside of the ladyfingers.

5. Pour about one-third of the raspberry mousse, in the bottom and spread it out evenly with an offset spatula.

6. Place 10–15 raspberries all over the surface of the mousse. Place them strategically so when eating the charlotte there are raspberries in every bite. Top the raspberries with a few tablespoons of mousse. Spread the mousse so the raspberries are covered with a nice flat surface. Place in the freezer for 15 minutes.

Recipe continued on page 144.

7. Place the second ladyfinger disk on top of the mousse add 12–15 raspberries, top with a few tablespoons of mousse, and place back in the freezer for 15 minutes.

8. Spread the remaining mousse on top and freeze again for 20 minutes.

9. Decorate the top with the remaining raspberries in concentric circles so none of the cream is visible. Refrigerate the charlotte for 12 hours.

10. Gently unmold the cake and tie a ribbon around the outside, if desired. If making a jam glaze, in a microwave-safe bowl, add the jam and heat for 20 seconds. Using a pastry brush, brush a thin layer of jam all over the raspberries to give them a nice shiny look. Serve immediately.

11. Store in an airtight container in the refrigerator for up to 2 days.

Variations

You can make this dessert with any fresh fruit you like; strawberries or pears are also delicious.

French Beignets

Light fluffy clouds of dough lightly coated in sugar—is there anything better? I love that every country around the world has their own variation of fried dough covered in powdered sugar; the shape and texture change, but the comfort from this dessert remains. The traditional beignets from New Orleans are very different in texture from French beignets, which are a bit thicker and denser and less sweet. These are the perfect snack, and the dough is wonderful with all kinds of different flavors and fillings.

Yield: 12 beignets

Prep Time: 25 minutes

Rest Time: 4 hours or overnight

Cooking Time: 2–3 minutes each

Difficulty: Easy

Tools: stand mixer, rubber spatula, rolling pin, 4-inch (10-cm) round cookie cutter, instant-read thermometer, chopsticks, sifter

1. In a 2-qt (1.8-L) saucepan, warm the milk over low heat until lightly warm not hot. In a small bowl, add the yeast and warm milk. Mix together and set aside for 10 minutes to autolyze the yeast to make sure it is active and ready to use (page 25).

2. In the bowl of a stand mixer fitted with a hook attachment, add the egg yolks, egg, granulated sugar, melted butter, oil, and vanilla. Mix to combine.

3. Add two-thirds of the flour and knead on medium speed for 8 minutes.

- 7 g (2¼ teaspoons or 1 packet) active dry yeast
- 180 ml (¾ cup) whole milk
- 40 g (2) egg yolks, at room temperature
- 50 g (1) egg, at room temperature
- 50 g (¼ cup) granulated sugar
- 70 g (5 tablespoons) unsalted butter, melted and cooled
- 30 ml (2 tablespoons) grapeseed oil or neutral oil, plus more for the bowl
- 9 g (2 teaspoons) vanilla bean paste
- 400 g (3⅓ cups) all-purpose flour, plus more for dusting
- 500 ml (2⅓ cups) peanut oil or frying oil
- Powdered sugar, for dusting

Chef Tips

Allow the beignets to rise and double in volume to make sure they are fluffy. Do not overheat the frying oil or they will get very dark. The dough can be made in advance and stored in the refrigerator overnight.

4. Add the yeast mixture and the remaining one-third of flour. Knead on medium speed for 10 minutes longer, until the dough is shiny and smooth. Complete the windowpane test (page 25) to make sure it is ready for proofing and will make nice, fluffy beignets.

5. Lightly oil a large bowl, place the dough in the bowl, turn to coat, and cover with a clean kitchen towel. Let proof for 2 hours, until doubled in size. If making the dough in advance, place in the refrigerator to retard the dough and slow the proofing process until ready to fry.

6. Turn out the dough onto a lightly floured work surface. Roll out the dough until about ½ inch (1.3 cm) thick (if the dough is too thin, the beignets will be flat). Using a 4-inch (10-cm) round cookie cutter, cut out the beignets. Press down on the dough without twisting the cookie cutter. Twisting the cookie cutter will seal the layers and not allow them to rise properly.

7. Cut 12 squares of parchment paper and place each beignet on its own paper square. Place them all on a baking sheet and proof for 2 hours longer, until doubled in size. They may need more time to ensure they are double in size; this is the key to achieving a nice, fluffy result.

8. Add the oil to a 4-qt (3.6-l) saucepan and heat to 325°F (160°C) on an instant-read thermometer. Line a plate with paper towels.

9. Slide one beignet at a time into the oil using the parchment paper square to maintain their form. Fry each beignet for 2–3 minutes on each side, using chopsticks to rotate them in the oil, until evenly golden brown. Transfer them to the prepared plate to absorb any excess oil. Dust with powdered sugar and serve immediately.

Variations

Fill with your favorite jam or chocolate spread.

Churro Bites

Originating in Portugal and Spain, churros are little bites of heaven. They are made from a variation of pâte à choux dough, fried, and then rolled in cinnamon sugar. It is common to serve them with all sorts of dipping sauces, such as melted chocolate, dulce de leche, or a favorite jam. They come together very quickly, with no proofing time required.

Yield: 30–40 churro bites

Prep Time: 15 minutes (plus master recipe)

Cook Time: 2–3 minutes each

Difficulty: Easy

Tools: Piping bag, star tip, instant-read thermometer, kitchen scissors, sifter

1 batch Pâte à Choux Dough (page 38)

500 ml (2¼ cups) peanut oil or frying oil

For Dusting

80 g (⅓ cup) granulated sugar

10 g (1 tablespoon) ground cinnamon

1. Fit a piping bag with a star tip and add the pâte à choux dough. Line a plate with paper towels.

2. In a 3-qt (2.7-l) saucepan, add the oil and heat to 325°F (160°C) on an instant-read thermometer. Drop a small piece of dough into the oil to make sure the oil is hot enough. The oil should bubble around the churro and make it puff up quickly. The dough will begin to get light golden brown.

3. Pipe bite-size portions of dough into the oil, using kitchen scissors to cut off the pieces. Fry until lightly golden brown, 2–3 minutes. Place on the prepared plate to absorb any excess oil.

4. To dust the churro bites: In a bowl, combine the sugar and cinnamon and dust all over the churro bites. Serve immediately. Churros taste best fresh, so do not store. The dough in the piping bag can rest for 2–3 hours, at the most, in advance of frying them.

My Famous Tarte Tatin (the French Version of Apple Pie)

Obsessed with perfecting this recipe the past ten years would be understating how incredible this dessert is. You may want to eat the entire thing in one sitting. The apples cook slowly in a buttery caramel until they are completely translucent, while resting on a bed of caramelized extra-flaky puff pastry. Like most French recipes, this one was created by accident when a pastry chef spilled the tart and it flipped upside down. Now pastry chefs around the world have interpreted their own version of this classic. You can also replace the apples with other fruits like peaches, nectarines, and pears, although the original version strictly uses apples. I recommend using Honeycrisp apples, as they hold up the best in the oven.

Yield: One 9-inch (23-cm) tart, 8 servings

Prep Time: 40 minutes (plus master recipes)

Bake Time: 35–45 minutes

Difficulty: Intermediate

Tools: 9-inch (23-cm) cake pan, rubber spatula, candy thermometer, balloon whisk, paring knife, pastry brush

For the Tatin

300 g (1½ cups) granulated sugar

100 ml (½ cup) water

113 g (½ cup) unsalted butter, at room temperature

6 Honeycrisp apples

For the Puff Pastry

1 sheet Rough Puff Pastry (page 33) or store-bought

30 g (2 tablespoons) granulated sugar

For the Quick Egg Wash

50 g (1) egg

20 ml (4 teaspoons) heavy cream

Crème fraîche, for serving

1. Preheat the oven to 350°F (175°C). Set a 9-inch (23-cm) cake pan on a baking sheet.

2. To make the tatin: In a 3- or 4-qt (2.7- or 3.6-l) saucepan, add the sugar and water. Run your rubber spatula through to make sure the sugar is completely covered by the water and won't stick to the bottom of the pot. Bring to a boil over medium-high heat. Once the mixture begins to boil *do not stir*. Let it cook to a light amber color, 311°F–329°F (155°C–165°C) on a candy thermometer. Reduce the heat to medium and whisk in the butter with a balloon whisk, 14 g (1 tablespoon) at a time, whisking in between each addition. The caramel should be perfectly smooth and combined. Pour the caramel into the bottom of the cake pan. Angle the pan so caramel coats the bottom evenly all over. Set aside for 20 minutes, until hardened.

3. Peel and core the apples. Cut them into quarters or halves. If using quartered apples, arrange them in a concentric circle covering the caramel. If using halved apples, place them in a clockface with the cut side facing up.

4. Next, roll out the puff pastry on a piece of parchment paper. Cut out a 9-inch (23-cm) circle with a paring knife. Dock a few holes in the dough with a fork and place over the apples.

5. To make the egg wash: In a small bowl, whisk together the egg and heavy cream. Brush the egg wash over the puff pastry evenly and dust with the 30 g (2 tablespoons) of sugar.

6. Bake for 35–45 minutes, until the apples and caramel are bubbling along the edges of the pan and the puff pastry is perfectly golden brown all over. Remove from the oven and let cool for 5 minutes.

7. Line a baking sheet with a cooling rack. Carefully unmold the tart onto the cooling rack. There may be some juice, so watch your hands as you flip the tart over onto the cooling rack. Let it cool for 15 minutes and enjoy warm. Serve with crème fraîche for the perfect pairing of sweet and tart. This dessert doesn't keep well because the apples soften the puff pastry within a few hours. Enjoy fresh.

Pear Almond Galette
(Amandine aux Poires)

This is a personal favorite and an homage to my mom, who is obsessed with all things almond cream. It is a classic French dessert you will spot in most patisseries around Paris, and France. The baked almond cream offers a light, fluffy texture on the inside. The pears bring just the right amount of sweetness and elegance, and, with the added crunch from the sweet dough, it's perfection in every bite. Simple and elegant, this one is always a crowd-pleaser.

Yield: One 10-inch (25-cm) galette

Prep Time: 25 minutes
(plus master recipes)

Bake Time: 30–35 minutes

Chill Time: 1 hour

Difficulty: Easy

Tools: Silicone mat, rolling pin, piping bag, offset spatula, balloon whisk, pastry brush, sifter

For the Galette

1 batch Sweet Pastry Dough
(page 32), chilled

All-purpose flour, for dusting

½ batch Almond Cream
(page 49), chilled

4 large Bostock pears, poached in
Poaching Liquid for Stone Fruits
(page 60)

For the Quick Egg Wash

50 g (1) whole egg

20 ml (4 teaspoons) heavy cream

For Decorating

40 g (⅔ cup) sliced almonds

30 g (¼ cup) powdered sugar

Chef Tips

Seal the almond cream with the dough all along the edges to keep it from spreading too much in the oven. You can also make eight small galettes instead of one large one to serve individually.

1. Preheat the oven to 350°F (175°C). Line a sheet pan with a silicone mat.

2. To make the galette: Dust your rolling pin with flour (this dough is sticky). On a silicone mat, roll out the dough to ¼ inch (6 mm) thick and 10–11 inches (25–28 cm) in diameter. This dessert does not need to be baked in a dish because galettes are baked free-form directly on a silicone mat on a baking sheet.

3. Load the chilled almond cream into a piping bag (no tip required). Pipe the cream starting from the center and moving out in a spiral. Spread it out evenly with an offset spatula, leaving 2- to 3-inch (5- to 7.5-cm) border around the edge.

4. Cut the poached pears in half or slice and arrange them on the almond cream. Push them in lightly so they bake nicely in the almond cream. Be sure to remove the core if you poached them whole. Fold the pastry dough back over the edge of the almond cream to create a border and seal in the cream.

5. To make the egg wash: In a bowl, combine the egg and heavy cream and mix together until smooth, about 2 minutes.

6. Brush the edges of the galette with the egg wash and dust with the sliced almonds.

7. Slide the galette onto a baking sheet without lifting the silicone mat and bake for 30 minutes, until the edges are completely golden brown and the top is lightly golden brown.

8. Remove the galette from the oven and let cool to room temperature. Dust with powdered sugar and serve immediately.

9. Store in an airtight container at room temperature for up to 2 days.

Fresh Strawberry Tart
(Tarte aux Fraises)

A light sweet crumbly dough, a thin layer of strawberry jam, a filling of vanilla bean pastry cream, and a topping of fresh strawberries make this the perfect recipe to celebrate strawberry season. This simple and elegant tart will dress up the table and be the hit of the event every time; it's perfect to serve at both lunch and dinner.

Yield: One 8-inch (20-cm) tart

Prep Time: 45 minutes (plus master recipes)

Bake Time: 20 minutes

Chill Time: 1 hour

Difficulty: Easy

Tools: silicone mat, rolling pin, baking beans, balloon whisk, piping bag, offset spatula, pastry brush

For the Tart

½ batch Sweet Tart Dough (page 32), chilled

120 g (¾ cup) strawberry jam, divided

½ batch Pastry Cream (page 44), chilled

450 g (1 lb) fresh strawberries

For Decoration

50 g (½ cup) crushed pistachios

1. Preheat the oven to 350°F (175°C). Brush an 8-inch (20-cm) tart ring with butter and place it on a baking sheet lined with a silicone mat or parchment paper.

2. On a piece of parchment paper, roll out the dough into a 9-inch (23-cm) circle ¼ inch (6 mm) thick. Dust the rolling pin lightly with flour to prevent sticking. Flip the dough circle onto the ring and slowly peel back the parchment paper. Press the dough into the tart ring on the bottom and along the sides, then trim off any excess that comes up over the edges. Cover with parchment paper and fill with raw beans, uncooked rice, or baking beads as a weight. Blind bake for 15 minutes. Remove the weights and bake uncovered for 5 minutes longer. The tart shell should be fully cooked and perfectly golden brown. Allow the tart shell to cool completely.

3. Evenly spread half the jam on the bottom of the tart shell.

4. In a bowl, whisk the pastry cream to loosen it up and load it into a piping bag (no need for a piping tip). Pipe the pastry cream to the edge of the shell. Using an offset spatula, spread the pastry cream evenly; it should come about three-quarters of the way up the sides. Pinch your thumb and index finger together and run them all along the edge of the tart to remove any excess pastry cream.

5. Slice the strawberries in half as evenly as you can. Line the cut strawberries along the edge of the tart facing in the same direction. Make a second row inside the first in the opposite direction. Repeat, switching directions for each row.

6. In a microwave-safe bowl, add the remaining half of the strawberry jam and heat for 20 seconds. Using a pastry brush, brush the jam on the strawberries to give them a nice shiny finish. Top with the crushed pistachios for a little color. Refrigerate for 1 hour before serving.

7. Store in an airtight container in the refrigerator for up to 2 days.

XL Queen of Hearts
(Palmier Géant)

These large, flaky puff pastry hearts with just the right amount of sweetness are baked to represent the palm leaf shape. This nostalgic pastry is a childhood favorite of many, and it exists in different varieties in many cultures around the world.

Yield: 8 large palmiers

Prep Time: 15 minutes

Chill Time: 20 minutes

Bake Time: 20–22 minutes

Difficulty: Intermediate

Tools: Silicone mat, chef's knife, sifter, spatula

50 g (¼ cup) granulated sugar

1 sheet Rough Puff Pastry (page 33) or store-bought

30 g (¼ cup) powdered sugar

Chef Tips

The trick is to get these very caramelized. Be sure to flip them halfway through the baking process. Dust them with powdered sugar. Freeze the hearts as you preheat the oven to keep that shape intact.

1. Dust your work surface with the granulated sugar. Keep the paton of puff pastry in the same shape once you have completed all of the turns. Fold the edges toward the center so they meet in the middle. Fold again on top of the same fold to have a double flap on each side meet in the middle. Place the heart log in the freezer for 20 minutes.

2. Preheat the oven to 375°F (190°C). Line a baking sheet with a silicone mat or parchment paper.

3. Remove the dough from the freezer and use a sharp chef's knife to slice hearts ¼–½ inch (6–13 mm) thick. Place them on the prepared baking sheet, and space them out evenly so they have room to finish expanding in the oven. Dust the hearts with half the powdered sugar.

4. Transfer the baking sheet to the center rack and bake for 10 minutes. Remove from the oven and use a spatula to flip the hearts over. Dust with the remaining powdered sugar and place back in the oven for 10–12 more minutes, until golden brown and a little darker around the edges than the middle. Remove from the oven and let cool to room temperature.

5. Store in an airtight bag for up to 5 days. Store the unbaked log in the freezer wrapped in parchment paper and plastic wrap for up to 2 weeks.

Variations

Dust the hearts with cinnamon sugar or dip them in chocolate once cooled. For a savory option, coat the baking sheet with butter and sprinkle Gruyère cheese over the hearts.

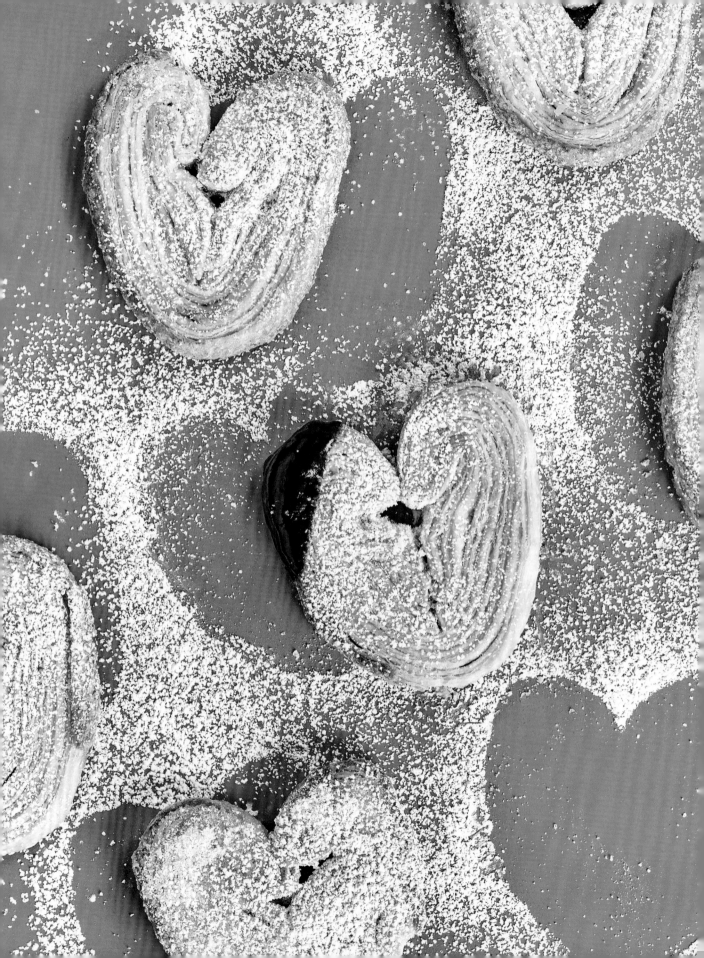

Mocha Cake (Gâteau Moka)

Coffee lovers, rejoice. This cake is for you. The flavors of coffee, chocolate, vanilla, and butter prove that the whole is greater than the sum of its parts in this delicious combination. The creamy frosting binds the cake together into the perfect bite, and toasted almonds tie it all together. Of course, you'll want to enjoy a slice with coffee!

Yield: One 6-inch (15-cm) cake

Prep Time: 25 minutes
(plus master recipe)

Chill Time: 1 hour

Difficulty: Intermediate

Tools: Stand mixer, rubber spatula, piping bag, star tip, offset spatula, serrated knife

For the Cake

2 batches Genoise (page 30)

For the Buttercream Frosting

227 g (1 cup) unsalted butter, at room temperature

340 g (3 cups) powdered sugar

9 g (2 teaspoons) vanilla bean paste

80 ml (⅓ cup) whole milk, at room temperature

30 ml (2 tablespoons) espresso, at room temperature

60 g (⅓ cup) dark chocolate chips

100 g (1½ cups) sliced almonds, lightly toasted

Chef Tips

- For an extra coffee flavor, make a coffee simple syrup and brush it on each cake layer before frosting.
- To toast the almonds, place them on a baking sheet and bake at 350°F (175°C) for 15 minutes until light golden brown.

1. To make the buttercream frosting: In the bowl of a stand mixer fitted with a paddle attachment, add the butter, 170 g (1½ cups) of the powdered sugar, the vanilla, and 40 ml (2 tablespoons + 2 teaspoons) of the milk. Beat on high speed for 10 minutes. Scrape down the sides of the bowl and beat for 5 minutes longer. Add the remaining 170 g (1½ cups) of sugar, the remaining 40 ml (2 tablespoons + 2 teaspoons) of milk, and the espresso shot and beat for 10 minutes longer. The buttercream should be super creamy, doubled in size, light, and very fluffy. If not, mix for 10 minutes longer. All the flavor for this cake comes from the buttercream, so get that perfectly mixed together.

2. In a microwave-safe bowl, add the dark chocolate chips and melt in the microwave in 20-second increments, stirring in between each interval, until completely melted. Stir with a spatula to cool it down. As you continue to whip the buttercream frosting, stream in the room temperature melted chocolate and beat for 5 minutes longer. Load the frosting into a piping bag fitted with a star tip and set aside.

3. Set up your station with your genoises, buttercream, offset spatula, and sliced almonds. With a serrated knife, cut each genoise in half horizontally, creating two layers per cake. You should have a total of four layers. Pipe a small amount of frosting on a cake stand or serving plate to act as the glue and set down the first cake layer. Pipe frosting on the cake layer, spread it around with your offset spatula, and stack the next one evenly on top; repeat to use all the cake layers. Be sure to reserve enough buttercream for the outside of the cake. Apply a thin coat of frosting to the outside of the cake as a crumb coat. Refrigerate the cake for 30 minutes.

4. Pipe the rest of the frosting along the outside and spread it evenly with an offset spatula to cover the outside of the cake evenly. Pipe eight rosettes along the top edge of the cake.

5. Decorate the cake with the toasted sliced almonds. Chill in the refrigerator for 30 minutes and serve cold.

6. Store in an airtight container the refrigerator for up to 5 days.

Giant Frosted Choco Tart

Welcome to the homemade gourmet version of the all-time classic favorite packaged breakfast pastry. This one is leveled up with a baked chocolate ganache, creamy royal icing, and gorgeous sprinkles. It comes together quickly and will become a beloved weekend bake. Have fun replacing the filling with any of your favorites, such as jam, chocolate spread, or a flavored ganache.

Yield: One 10 by 12-inch (25 by 30-cm) tart, 6 servings

Prep Time: 30 minutes (plus master recipes)

Bake Time: 20–25 minutes

Difficulty: Easy

Tools: Silicone mat, rolling pin, paring knife, piping bag, offset spatula, fork, pastry brush, balloon whisk

For the Choco Tart

1 batch Easy Flaky Crust (page 36), chilled

1 batch Ganache 2:1 Ratio (page 54)

For the Quick Egg Wash

50 g (1) whole egg

20 ml (4 teaspoons) heavy cream

For the Icing

120 g (1 cup) powdered sugar

130 ml (2 tablespoons) heavy cream

40 g (⅓ cup) sprinkles

1. Preheat the oven to 350°F (175°C). Line a baking sheet with a silicone mat or parchment paper.

2. Divide the chilled tart dough in half. Work the dough quickly with your hands to make it pliable, about 2 minutes if the dough was chilled overnight. Place the dough in the center of the prepared baking sheet and roll it into a large rectangle roughly 10 x 12 inches (25 x 30 cm) about ¼ inch (6 mm) thick. Use a lightly floured rolling pin to prevent the dough from sticking. Use a paring knife to fix the edges so they are as even as possible.

3. Roll out the second half of the dough the exact same way on another sheet of parchment paper or a silicone mat. Pipe or spoon the ganache in the middle of the tart and spread it evenly with an offset spatula, leaving a 2- to 3-inch (5- to 7.5-cm) border around the edge.

4. To make the egg wash: In a small bowl, combine the egg and heavy cream. Mix together with a fork for 30 seconds until smooth.

5. Brush the edges of the bottom of the tart with the egg wash. Cover the tart with the top piece of dough. Press a fork around the edges to seal the two pieces of dough together. Brush the top with egg wash twice.

6. Bake for 20–25 minutes, until golden brown. Remove from the oven and let cool completely on a wire rack.

7. To make the icing: In a small bowl, add the powdered sugar and heavy cream and whisk until smooth, 1 minute. Pour on top of the large choco tart and spread with an offset spatula to make sure the icing is even. Wait 2–3 minutes for the icing to set a little so the sprinkles don't sink. Top with the sprinkles.

8. Store in an airtight container at room temperature for up to 4 days. Do not freeze.

Variations

Add 30 g (2 tablespoons) of strawberry preserves to the ganache for a chocolaty berry version.

XL Fresh Strawberry Choux to Share *(Choux à la Fraise)*

If you are looking for an impressive elegant dessert to dress up a party or special event, this is it. On a bed of golden choux puffs lies an incredibly rich, light and creamy crème légère. This dessert is wonderful to serve after a heavy meal and great all summer long to dress up those barbecues. It's a showstopper for sure.

Yield: One 10-inch (25-cm) choux puff, 4–6 servings

Prep Time: 30 minutes (plus master recipes)

Bake Time: 25 to 30 minutes

Chill Time: 1 hour

Difficulty: Intermediate

Tools: Silicone mat, piping bag, fork, round tip, pastry brush, serrated knife, sifter, offset spatula

1 batch Pâte à Choux Dough (page 36), unbaked

For the Quick Egg Wash

50 g (1) egg

20 ml (4 teaspoons) heavy cream

1 batch Crème Légère (page 45)

200 g (1 cup) fresh strawberries, tops removed

Powdered sugar, for dusting

1. Preheat the oven to 350°F (175°C). Line a baking sheet with a silicone mat or parchment paper.

2. Load the choux dough into a piping bag (no tip needed). On the prepared baking sheet, pipe the choux dough in two rows of six choux each, with the choux in each row next to one another so as they bake and expand they stick together. Reserve any remaining choux for another recipe.

3. To make the egg wash: In a small bowl, combine the egg and heavy cream. Mix together with a fork for 30 seconds until smooth. Spread evenly over the choux.

4. Bake for 20 to 25 minutes until dark golden brown. Remove from the oven and let cool to room temperature.

5. Load the crème légère into a piping bag fitted with a round tip. Cut the strawberries into eighths so they are thin and pointy.

6. Use a serrated knife to cut the choux rows in half horizontally, keeping them together. Set the top of the choux to the side. Place the bottom halves on a serving platter and pipe the crème légère in tall round dollops.

7. Place the strawberries on the outside of the cream all around the choux. Angle them in different directions and use the cream to stick them to the dessert.

8. Dust the top of the choux with powdered sugar. Using an offset spatula, gently place the hats back onto the base of the choux puffs, covering the cream.

9. Refrigerate for 1 hour before serving.

10. Store in an airtight container in the refrigerator for up to 2 days.

Quick Treats

This section is dedicated to quick and easy treats that taste like you spent hours in the kitchen. These sweet treats, snackables, and simple desserts will all make you look like a rock star. Most quick desserts consist of hacks, such as fake ice creams (frozen whipped cream), but these recipes are all very reliable and use French baking techniques to make you look like a pro. These are some of my favorite desserts reinvented in a quick format, so they take half the time, but are definitely not half the quality. These are the perfect treats to throw together on those busy days, but they will still impress your guests and create special moments. This chapter is filled with delicious desserts, snacks, pastries that you can make, for the most part, in under an hour. So, level up your snack game and elevate your taste buds with these treats.

Mini Apple Turnovers
(Chaussons aux Pommes)

This pastry originated in Saint-Calais in the northwest region of France. The story goes that as a way of combatting a hunger epidemic back in 1630s, the government handed out hundreds of "pâte aux pommes," apples in a sweet tart dough that were dense and heavy and meant to keep you full for several hours. Since then, this pastry has been refined and redefined as a staple French pastry.

Yield: 12–16 mini turnovers

Prep Time: 20 minutes
(plus master recipe)

Chill Time: 10 minutes

Bake Time: 15–20 minutes

Difficulty: Easy

Tools: Silicone mat, peeler, corer, paring knife, 4-inch (10-cm) round cookie cutter, balloon whisk, pastry brush

For the Apple Filling

8 Honeycrisp apples, peeled, cored, and diced into small cubes (brunoise)

30 g (2 tablespoons) granulated sugar

50 g (¼ cup) light brown sugar

27 g (2 tablespoons) unsalted butter

80 ml (⅓ cup) water

9 g (2 teaspoons) vanilla bean paste

For the Puff Pastry

1 sheet Rough Puff Pastry (page 33), unbaked, or store-bought

45 g (3 tablespoons) granulated sugar

For the Quick Egg Wash

50 g (1) whole egg

20 ml (4 teaspoons) heavy cream

For the Topping

40 g (3 tablespoons) raw cane sugar

1. Preheat the oven to 350°F (175°C). Line a baking sheet with a silicone mat or parchment paper.

2. To make the apple filling: Place the diced apples in a 3-qt (2.7-l) saucepan. Add the granulated sugar, brown sugar, butter, water, and vanilla. Cover and cook over medium-low heat, stirring occasionally to ensure nothing sticks to the bottom. Cook for about 15 minutes, until translucent and lightly golden brown. Set aside.

3. To prepare the puff pastry: On your work surface, lay out the sheet of puff pastry. Dust both sides with the granulated sugar. Using a 4-inch (10-cm) cookie cutter, cut out circles from the pastry. Place the circles on the prepared baking sheet, spacing them out evenly. Spoon a small amount of the apple filling on one side of each circle, leaving a ½-inch (1.3-cm) border.

4. To make the egg wash: In a small bowl, whisk together the egg and cream. Brush the outer edge of each circle with a small amount of egg wash. Fold one side over the filling and press around the perimeter with your fingers to seal the edges. Brush just the top with egg wash and dust with a little raw cane sugar. Place the baking sheet in the freezer for 10 minutes.

5. Remove the turnovers from the freezer and brush the top one last time with the egg wash and sprinkle with the raw cane sugar. Bake for 15–20 minutes, or until golden brown. DO NOT open the oven for the first 15 minutes to ensure they rise properly. Serve warm or at room temperature.

6. Store in an airtight container for up to 2 days. The dough will soften, so simply place it back in the oven for a few minutes before serving to get the puff pastry nice and crispy.

OPPOSITE PAGE (top to bottom): Mini Swiss Pastries (page 166), Apple Turnovers, Mini Almond Puff Pastry Boats (page 167)

Mini Swiss Pastries
(Pains Suisse)

Growing up in Paris, my grandmother would always bring one of these or a pain au chocolate after school. It is one of my absolute favorite pastries. A golden layer of puff pastry wraps around creamy vanilla pastry cream and dark chocolate chips. Crunchy, creamy, decadent, and lightly chocolaty, this one hits all the marks. It can be made with either brioche dough or puff pastry.

Yield: 12 mini pastries

Prep Time: 30 minutes
(plus master recipes)

Bake Time: 15–20 minutes

Chill Time: 15 minutes

Difficulty: Intermediate

Tools: Silicone mat, paring knife, balloon whisk, piping bag, pastry brush

For the Puff Pastry

1 sheet Rough Puff Pastry (page 33), unbaked, or store-bought 45g (3 tablespoons) granulated sugar

For the Filling

½ batch Pastry Cream (page 44), chilled

100 g (⅔ cup) mini chocolate chips

For the Quick Egg Wash

50 g (1) egg

45 ml (3 tablespoons) heavy cream

1. Preheat the oven to 350°F (175°C). Line a baking sheet with a silicone mat or parchment paper.

2. To prepare the puff pastry: Place the puff pastry on your work surface and dust both sides with the sugar. Cut six long strips vertically from the sheet, then cut across horizontally to create 12 small rectangles.

3. To make the filling: Place the chilled pastry cream in a bowl and whisk with a balloon whisk to loosen it, then fold in the chocolate chips. Load the pastry cream into a piping bag without a piping tip. Pipe a small amount in the center of each rectangle.

4. To make the egg wash: In a small bowl, whisk together the egg and heavy cream. Brush on the outside border of each pastry and fold over to seal the edges. Brush the top of each pastry. Do not brush the edges as this will cause the layers to seal together. Place them on the prepared baking sheet and chill in the freezer for 15 minutes.

5. Brush the tops of each pastry once more with egg wash, then bake for 15–20 minutes, until dark golden brown. Remove from the oven and let cool for 15 minutes.

6. Store an airtight container at room temperature for up to 3 days. These can also be assembled and frozen without the egg wash for 2 weeks. To bake from frozen, brush with the egg wash and simply add a few minutes to the baking time.

Mini Almond Puff Pastry Raspberry Boats
(Barquettes aux Framboises)

Flaky, buttery puff pastry is filled with a thin layer of almond cream and fresh raspberries in this elegant and delicious dessert. They are both sweet and tart and come together very quickly using the rough puff pastry recipe in the book or your favorite store-bought puff pastry.

Yield: 12–16 pastries

Prep Time: 10 minutes (plus master recipes)

Bake Time: 15–20 minutes

Chill Time: 15 minutes

Difficulty: Easy

Tools: Silicone mat, stand mixer, rolling pin, 4-inch (10-cm) round cookie cutter, balloon whisk, pastry brush, piping bag

For the Filling

1 batch Almond Cream (page 49), chilled

24–32 fresh raspberries

For the Puff Pastry

1 sheet Rough Puff Pastry (page 33), unbaked, or store-bought

45 g (3 tablespoons) granulated sugar

For the Quick Egg Wash

50 g (1) egg

45 ml (3 tablespoons) heavy cream

Powdered sugar, for dusting

1. Preheat the oven to 350°F (175°C). Line a baking sheet with a silicone mat or parchment paper. Set out a piping bag with no tip.

2. To make the filling: In the bowl of a stand mixer fitted with a paddle attachment, add the almond cream. Whip for 1 minute to make sure it's smooth.

3. To prepare the puff pastry: On your work surface, lay out the sheet of puff pastry. Dust each side with the granulated sugar and use a rolling pin to push the sugar into the dough. Using a 4-inch (10-cm) cookie cutter, cut out the puff pastry rounds. Push straight down and do not twist the cookie cutter, as this can seal the layers and keep the dough from rising. Using the scraps of the dough around the circle outline, cut thin strips to use as borders for each pastry round. You should get 12 to 16 rounds.

4. To make the egg wash: In a small bowl, add the egg and heavy cream. Whisk to combine. Brush the edge of each pastry circle with the egg wash, then place a thin strip of puff pastry all the way around, creating a border. Using a fork, dock a few holes in the center of the dough. Place each on on the prepared baking sheet.

5. Pipe a dollop of almond cream in the middle (about 30 g [2 tablespoons]) and place two or three fresh raspberries in the center of each one, depending on size. Chill in the freezer for 15 minutes.

6. Brush each top border with a little more egg wash and bake for 15–20 minutes, until the edges are golden brown. Allow to cool room temperature, dust with a little powdered sugar, and serve immediately.

7. Store in an airtight container at room temperature for up to 3 days. Reheat in the oven at 300°F (150°C) for several minutes before serving to crisp up the dough. These can also be stored in the freezer with the egg wash and baked right from frozen. Simply add a few minutes to the baking time.

Pantry Chocolaty Snack Mix

Crunchy, sweet, salty, and chewy, this snack mix hits all the right textures. Pantries can get overcrowded, and this recipe is one sure way to use up those half-empty boxes of cereal or pretzels left behind. Imagine rocky road in snack mix form. This is the perfect snack to have on hand for a late-night chocolate craving and is packed full of nuts, cereals, and a surprise in every bite.

Yield: 870 g (30 oz), 6 servings

Prep Time: 10 minutes

Chill Time: 2 hours

Difficulty: Easy

Tools: Spatula, silicone mat

- 150 g (3 cups) Chex mix cereal
- 84 g (2 cups) pretzel sticks, broken into bite-size pieces
- 150 g (3 cups) cinnamon crunch cereal
- 50 g (⅓ cup) toasted unsalted peanuts
- 50 g (⅓ cup) toasted unsalted almonds
- 100 g (2 cups) mini marshmallows
- 240 g (1½ cups) dark chocolate chips
- 100 g (1 cup) powdered sugar

1. In a mixing bowl, add the Chex, pretzels, cinnamon crunch cereal, peanuts, almonds, and marshmallows. Stir to combine.

2. In a small microwave-safe bowl, add the chocolate chips and melt in 20-second increments, stirring in between each interval, until completely melted. The chocolate should be melted, but not hot. If it is very warm, mix it for 1–2 minutes to cool it down. Pour the chocolate over the cereal and nut mixture. Toss so everything is completely coated.

3. Line a baking sheet with a silicone mat or parchment paper. Pour the cereal mix onto it and dust with ample powdered sugar. Everything should be evenly coated. Place the baking sheet in the refrigerator for 2 hours to allow it to set.

4. Pour the mix into airtight zip-top bags and store at room temperature for up to 1 week. Snack away!

Variations

Have fun trying different nut and cereal combinations, maintaining the same weights to keep the proportions of the recipe the same.

Chef Tips

Do not overheat the chocolate or it will soften the cereal. Simply melt in 20-second increments in the microwave and stir in between each time until completely melted. Use a high-quality dark chocolate for a smooth chocolate coating and the best results.

OPPOSITE PAGE (top to bottom): Salted Butter Caramel Popcorn (page 171), Krispy Coco Granola, (page 170), Pantry Chocolaty Snack Mix

Krispy Coco Granola

This a great recipe to play with and make your own using any dried fruits or nuts you have on hand. Homemade granola often gets soft or chewy after several days, but with my secret trick you'll have crispy granola for weeks. Folding whipped egg whites into the granola mix makes this granola light and crispy.

Yield: 800 g (29 oz)

Prep Time: 20 minutes

Bake Time: 25–30 minutes

Difficulty: Easy

Tools: Silicone mat, rubber spatula, stand mixer

180 g (2 cups) rolled oats

120 g (1 cup) slivered almonds

70 g (1 cup) shredded unsweetened coconut

125 g (⅓ cup) honey

80 g (⅓ cup) light brown sugar

113 g (½ cup) unsalted butter, cubed

90 g (3) egg whites, at room temperature

1. Preheat the oven to 325°F (160°C). Line a baking sheet with a silicone mat or parchment paper.

2. In a mixing bowl, add the rolled oats, almonds, and coconut. Stir with a rubber spatula to mix everything together.

3. In a 2-qt (1.8-l) saucepan, add the honey, brown sugar, and butter. Cook over medium heat, stirring with the spatula until completely melted. Once melted, allow the mixture come to a simmer and cook until it reaches a thick syrup consistency, 5–7 minutes. Pour the butter sugar syrup into the bowl of nuts and oats. Mix with the spatula to get everything properly coated.

4. In the bowl of a stand mixer fitted with a whisk attachment, add the room temperature egg whites and whip until medium peaks form, 5–7 minutes. Fold the egg whites into the granola mixture as you would with a mousse,, folding gently so as not to deflate the egg whites. These egg whites will evaporate in the oven and leave you with the crunchiest, crispiest granola for weeks after it bakes.

5. Pour the mixture onto the prepared baking sheet and bake for 20 minutes, mix the granola around on the baking sheet, and bake for 5–10 minutes longer. The mixture will still appear slightly wet. Remove the baking sheet from the oven and stir the granola every couple of minutes, until it reaches room temperature. It will get crispier as it cools.

6. Store in an airtight container at room temperature for up to 3 weeks.

Salted Butter Caramel Popcorn

When a French pastry chef takes on popcorn it becomes a work of art. A silky, salted butter caramel perfectly coats each popcorn kernel. The best part is, I give you the trick for making the crunchiest popcorn that will keep for days! No more soft popcorn after a few days or hours. Now, the challenge is to make it last that long. It is addictively delicious.

Yield: 400 g (14 oz)

Prep Time: 15 minutes

Bake Time: 20–25 minutes

Difficulty: Easy

Tools: Silicone mat, rubber spatula, candy thermometer, balloon whisk

240 g (1¼ cups) granulated sugar

50 g (2½ tablespoons) glucose or corn syrup

150 g (5½ oz) unpopped popcorn kernels

250 g (1 cup + 1 tablespoon) unsalted butter, at room temperature

5 g (1 teaspoon) flaky sea salt

Chef Tips

- Use a clean saucepan, as any impurities can cause the sugar to mass.
- Use fresh granulated sugar, not a clumpy old sugar.
- Do not stir the caramel once the sugar begins to boil. Allow it to cook and do not vary the stovetop temperature.

1. Preheat the oven to 350°F (175°C). Line a baking sheet with a silicone mat or parchment paper.

2. In a small 2-qt (1.8-l) nonstick saucepan, add the sugar, followed by the glucose, and then add water to come about ½ inch (1.3 cm) above the sugar. Set over medium-high heat and start cooking the caramel. Run your spatula through the mixture to make sure the sugar is completely coated in water and will not stick to the bottom. Once the sugar syrup begins to boil, DO NOT STIR.

3. Pop the popcorn in the microwave as you cook the sugar. Allow the sugar to cook to a light amber color, about 8 minutes, or 311°F–329°F (155°C–165°C) on a candy thermometer. From this point, the sugar will continue to darken very quickly, so reduce the heat and whisk in the butter, 14 g (1 tablespoon) at a time. Whisk continuously to keep the caramel smooth. Add the salt and whisk to combine.

4. Pour the popcorn into a large bowl, pour the caramel over the popcorn, and mix with a spatula until coated. Spread the popcorn out evenly on the prepared baking sheet.

5. Bake for 20–25 minutes, stirring the popcorn every 5 minutes. This will get each kernel perfectly coated and avoid any solid chunks of caramel sitting on the bottom. When completely golden brown, remove from the oven.

6. Allow the popcorn to cool completely and then package it in airtight baggies. Store at room temperature for up to 3 weeks.

Creamy Chocolate Truffles

Like many French classic desserts, this recipe was created by accident. In 1895, pastry chef and chocolatier Louis Dufour was lacking some chocolate to finish up his desserts. It was the holiday season, and he needed to think quickly. Refusing to ask for help from his culinary friends, he took it upon himself to create what would now be known as the classic chocolate truffle. He quickly combined melted chocolate, cocoa powder, and heavy cream to form balls, and to make them more visually appealing, he dipped each one into melted chocolate and, then rolled it in cocoa powder. This was also the beginning of chocolate ganache. In France, it is very common to gift these for the Christmas holidays, and I love having them on hand to serve with an espresso.

Yield: 20 truffles

Prep Time: 15 minutes

Rest Time: 30–60 minutes

Chill Time: 1 hour

Difficulty: Easy

Tools: Balloon whisk, silicone mat

120 ml (½ cup) heavy cream

9 g (2 teaspoons) vanilla bean paste

250 g (1½ cups) 70 percent dark chocolate chips

15 g (1 tablespoon) unsalted butter, at room temperature

200 g (1¾ cups) unsweetened cocoa powder

Chef Tips

- The most important ingredient here is chocolate, so use a high-quality dark chocolate. A low-quality chocolate will have more sugar and less cocoa in it, creating a grainy and rough texture. See page 13 for what I like to use.

- To make these the OG way, temper some dark chocolate and dip in each chocolate ganache ball. Then dip them right away in the cocoa powder. This will give you the perfect bite of soft and creamy, with a slight crunch from the chocolate shell and a little bitter from the cocoa powder.

1. In a small saucepan, add the heavy cream and vanilla. Bring to a high simmer over medium heat, about 5 minutes.

2. In a bowl, add the chocolate chips. Pour the hot cream over the chocolate chips. Let stand for 20 seconds to allow the chocolate to start melting. Using a balloon whisk, whisk the chocolate ganache together and create a silky smooth consistency and fully emulsified. The mixture will go from looking like chocolate milk to smooth shiny chocolate cream. Add the butter and whisk until shiny and combined.

3. Cover the chocolate ganache with plastic wrap, pushing the plastic wrap down onto the surface to prevent a skin from forming. Let sit at room temperature for 30–60 minutes, until it is firm enough to scoop out small balls with a spoon. You can also load the ganache into a piping bag and pipe them out when the ganache is more set.

4. Line a baking sheet with a silicone mat or parchment paper. Spread the cocoa powder on a plate.

5. Scoop out bite-size amounts of the ganache and roll them into perfect balls. You can wear gloves if you prefer not to get messy. Work quickly, so you don't melt the ganache with the heat of your hands.

6. Roll the balls in the cocoa powder until coated. Transfer to the prepared baking sheet and chill in the refrigerator for 1 hour to allow the truffles to set fully.

7. Store in an airtight jar in the refrigerator for up to 2 weeks. Take them out about 1 hour before serving them for optimal taste and texture.

Variations

You can substitute part of the weight of the heavy cream for liquors like Baileys Irish Cream, whiskey, or even Champagne.

OPPOSITE PAGE (left to right): Creamy Chocolate Truffles, Dark Chocolate Bark (page174), Swiss Rochers (page 175)

Dark Chocolate Bark

Chocolate bark can be intimidating to make, but with my quick chocolate tempering hack you'll make this one on repeat. Using a high-quality dark chocolate with at least 60 percent cocoa mass is very important to the success of this recipe, as anything under that will give you trouble. Chocolate with higher sugar and fat content will mass and have issues re-crystallizing and setting nicely. Play with the toppings and make this one the new favorite go-to snack. You can make the bark with your favorite chocolate and all of your favorite pantry nut mixes.

Yield: 500 g (18 oz)

Prep Time: 10 minutes

Difficulty: Easy

Tools: Spatula, silicone mat, 9-inch (23-cm) square pan, offset spatula

---

300 g (10½ oz) dark chocolate chips

50 g (⅓ cup) toasted unsalted almonds

50 g (⅓ cup) toasted unsalted hazelnuts

50 g (⅓ cup) dried cranberries

50 g (⅓ cup) shelled unsalted pistachios

2 g (¼ teaspoon) flaky sea salt (optional)

1. Temper the chocolate chips using the seeding method (page 26).

2. Line a 9-inch (23-cm) square baking dish with parchment paper. Pour in the melted chocolate and spread evenly with an offset spatula. Wait 2–3 minutes for the chocolate to go from shiny to matte as is starts to set, then evenly disperse all of the toppings on the chocolate. Finish with the flaky sea salt. Place in the refrigerator for 30 minutes to allow the bark to set completely if not already set.

3. Break into large pieces and store in an airtight container at room temperature for up to 2 weeks.

Variations

Have fun trying different nut and topping combinations, but maintain equal weights to keep the proportions of the recipe the same.

Swiss Rochers

Swiss rochers are so easy to make and you won't believe how delicious they are.
Gently toasted, caramelized almonds are coated in chocolate for a crunchy, sweet bite.
The very first rocher dates back to 1948 and became a worldwide success. This is a
simplified version of the traditional hazelnut praline rocher. I sold these in my bakery
for years, and they were always a favorite in our chocolate gift boxes.

Yield: 20–25 rochers
Prep Time: 10 minutes
Bake Time: 30 minutes
Chill Time: 3–4 hours
Difficulty: Easy
Tools: Rubber spatula, silicone mat

40 g (⅓ cup) powdered sugar

60 ml (¼ cup) water

150 g (1 cup) slivered almonds

220 g (1⅓ cups) dark chocolate
chips (at least 60% dark)

Chef Tips
*For a little extra beauty, brush the
rochers with edible gold dust or
gold leaf for a festive touch.*

1. Preheat the oven to 350°F (175°C). Line a baking sheet with
silicone mat or parchment paper.

2. In a small bowl, combine the powdered sugar and water
to make a syrup, add the slivered almonds, and mix with
the spatula to get them coated. Pour the almonds onto the
prepared baking sheet.

3. Bake for 30 minutes, tossing the almonds every 10 minutes
so they toast and caramelize evenly.

4. In a microwave-safe bowl, add two-thirds of the chocolate
chips. Melt in 30-second increments, mixing in between, until
fully melted. Do not melt for more than 30 seconds at a time or
you will risk burning the chocolate. Add the remaining one-
third of the chocolate chips a few chips at a time. This will
cool the chocolate back down, bringing it closer to tempered
chocolate range. Mix the chocolate in between each addition
to help melt the chips and create a nice shine to the chocolate.
This is known as the seeding method in chocolate tempering.

5. Once the slivered almonds are a nice golden brown and
candied, allow them to cool down slightly by moving them
around on the baking sheet for 5 minutes. Pour them into the
melted chocolate and mix until they are all properly coated.

6. Spoon out 15 g (1 tablespoon) of the mixture at a time onto
the second prepared baking sheet. Space them out 2–3 inches
(5–7.5 cm) apart. Place the baking sheet in the refrigerator for
3–4 hours, until the chocolate is set.

7. Store the rochers in an airtight baggie in the refrigerator for
up to 3 weeks. These are insanely delicious and addictive. Enjoy
them cold or take them out about 20 minutes before serving if
enjoying with coffee.

Variations
Substitute the slivered almonds for any nuts you like. I absolutely love these with
chopped hazelnuts or pistachios. If you would like to try these with milk chocolate
instead, I suggest melting over bain-marie, because it is much more difficult to
temper milk chocolate than dark chocolate due to the high sugar content.

Rum Nantes Cake
(Gâteau Nantais)

This cake is softer and fluffier than cotton. This cake dates back to 1800s, when fishermen would take these on the boats with them. Because their teeth were not in the best shape, they got used to dipping the cake in rum to make it even softer and easier to chew. Today the rum is key ingredient and remains a Belgian favorite. Of course, you can omit the rum or swap it for other extracts, but this cake is so good that there is a yearly world competition for the best recipe to this day.

Yield: One 6-inch (15-cm) cake, 6 servings

Prep Time: 20 minutes

Bake Time: 35–45 minutes

Difficulty: Easy

Tools: Stand mixer, 6-inch (15-cm) cake pan, offset spatula, balloon whisk, rubber spatula

For the Cake

113 g (½ cup) unsalted butter, at room temperature

125 g (⅔ cup) granulated sugar

1 vanilla bean, split and scraped

150 g (3) eggs, at room temperature

120 g (1¼ cups) almond flour

60 g (½ cup) all-purpose flour

20 ml (1 tablespoon) dark rum

For the Icing

220 g (2 cups) powdered sugar

30 ml (1½ tablespoons) rum or lemon juice

1. Preheat the oven to 350°F (175°C). Brush a 6-inch (15-cm) cake pan with butter and line the bottom with a round of parchment paper.

2. To make the cake: In the bowl of a stand mixer fitted with a paddle attachment, add the butter, granulated sugar, and vanilla bean seeds. Beat on high speed for 5 minutes, or until light and creamy. Scrape down the sides of the bowl and add the eggs one at time, mixing in between each addition, and beat for 5 minutes longer. Add the almond flour, all-purpose flour, and rum. Mix together to combine. The batter should be perfectly smooth.

3. Pour the batter into the prepared cake pan and bake for 35–45 minutes, until a toothpick inserted into the center comes out clean and the top is dark golden brown. DO NOT open the oven for the first 35 minutes or the cake can collapse. The only rising agent this cake has is the air incorporated into the butter and sugar; there is no baking powder, so we need the heat of the oven to really help with the rise of this cake. Allow the cake to cool for 10 minutes before unmolding it onto a cooling rack. Let cool completely.

4. To make the icing: In a bowl, add the powdered sugar and two-thirds of the rum. Mix slowly to get a thick white icing; it should be firm and not too runny. If you need a little more liquid, add the remaining rum to achieve the desired consistency.

5. Flip the cake upside down, remove the parchment round from the bottom, and use the flat bottom surface as the top of the cake. Set it on the plate you will serve the cake on because you won't be able to move the cake once the icing sets.

6. Pour the icing in the center and use an offset spatula to push it out to the edges. It shouldn't drip over the top, but just sit along the edge. Let the icing set for 15 minutes.

7. Store in an airtight container at room temperature for up to 3 days.

Mini Cake Popsicles

We all need a few sprinkles in life, and this soft, fluffy pound cake dipped in a dark, rich, crunchy chocolate coating topped with some gorgeous sprinkles is the definition of a party dessert! These cake popsicles are not only delicious, but also come together quickly with very few ingredients.

Yield: 6–8 mini cakes (80–100 g [3–3½ oz] each)

Prep Time: 25 minutes

Bake Time: 15–20 minutes

Chill Time: 3 hours

Difficulty: Easy

Tools: Stand mixer, cakesicle silicone mold, rubber spatula, acrylic sticks or popsicle sticks

For the Cakes

113 g (½ cup) unsalted butter, at room temperature

50 g (¼ cup) granulated sugar

50 g (¼ cup) light brown sugar

50 g (1) egg, at room temperature

20 g (1) egg yolk, at room temperature

150 g (1¼ cups) all-purpose flour

5 g (1 teaspoon) baking powder

30 ml (2 tablespoons) milk (if needed)

For the Chocolate Coating and Decorations

300 g (2 cups) dark chocolate chips

20 g (1½ tablespoons) coconut oil

80 g (½ cup) sprinkles

Chef Tips

Always heat your chocolate in increments of 20 seconds at a time to avoid burning the cocoa in the chocolate. See page 26 for information on tempering chocolate.

1. reheat the oven 350°F (175°C). Line two baking sheets with silicone mats or parchment paper.

2. To make the cake: In the bowl of a stand mixer fitted with a paddle attachment, add the butter, granulated sugar, and brown sugar. Mix together on high speed for 5 minutes, until light and creamy. Scrape down the sides of the bowl, add the egg, and mix for 2 minutes. Add the egg yolk and mix for 5 minutes longer, until smooth and fluffy.

3. In a separate bowl, stir together the flour and baking powder. Add to the butter mixture and mix for 2 minutes to combine. If the batter is a little too thick, add the milk to smooth out the batter.

4. Place the cakesicle mold on top of one of the baking sheets. Fill each cavity with the batter. Place the baking sheet on the center rack and bake for 15–20 minutes, until golden brown and detatched from the edges. Remove from the oven and let cool. Unmold the cakes and set them on a cooling rack.

5. To make the chocolate coating: In a microwave-safe bowl, add the dark chocolate chips and coconut oil. Melt in 20-second increments, stirring in between each interval, until completely melted and smooth.

6. Set out the same number of acrylic or popsicle sticks as you have cakes. Dip the tip into the chocolate and slide it into the base of a cake. Do this for each cake. Place on a second prepared baking sheet and refrigerate 10 minutes.

7. Reheat the chocolate to maintain it at a smooth, shiny consistency. Angle the bowl and dip each cake one at time to completely coat. Place back on the baking sheet and top with sprinkles while the chocolate is still wet and then refrigerate for 2–3 hours until completely set.

8. Store in an airtight container at room temperature for up to 4 days. You can also store them in the refrigerator.

Variations

Add 10 g (1 tablespoon) of cocoa powder and 15 ml (1 tablespoon) of milk to the cake batter for a chocolate cake.

Rich and Fluffy Chocolate Cake
with Magic Mascarpone Mousse and Marinated Berries

The texture of this cake is similar to flourless chocolate cake in richness but with the light and fluffy texture of a soufflé. There's also a reason I named this mascarpone mousse magical, because once you make it I guarantee you will want to put it on absolutely everything. It's light and airy like crème chantilly (whipped cream), but the mascarpone makes it much thicker, becoming pipeable and decadent. Several Parisian bakeries where I worked all swore by this mousse, with each chef creating their own version and flavor combinations. It is a staple in so many cakes and other desserts.

Yield: One 9-inch cake (23-cm), 8 servings

Prep Time: 35 minutes

Bake Time: 30–35 minutes

Chill Time: 30 minutes

Difficulty: Intermediate

Tools: 9-inch (23-cm) cake pan, stand mixer, piping bag, star tip, rubber spatula

For the Cake

150 g (1 cup) dark chocolate chips

170 g (¾ cup) unsalted butter, at room temperature

50 g (1) egg, at room temperature

60 g (3) egg yolks, at room temperature

140 g (⅔ cup) granulated sugar

180 g (6) egg whites, at room temperature

45 g (⅓ cup) all-purpose flour

30 g (¼ cup) cocoa powder

For the Magic Mascarpone Mousse

100 g (½ cup) mascarpone

200 ml (¾ cup) heavy cream

50 g (½ cup) powdered sugar

1 vanilla bean, split and scraped

1. Preheat the oven to 350°F (175°C). Brush a 9-inch (23-cm) cake pan with butter and line the bottom with a circle of parchment paper. Fit a piping bag with a star tip and set aside.

2. To make the cake: In a microwave-safe bowl, add the dark chocolate chips and butter. Melt in 20-second increments, stirring in between each interval, until completely melted. Set aside.

3. In a mixing bowl set over a bain-marie (water bath), add the egg, egg yolks, and 70 g (⅓ cup) of the granulated sugar. Whisk over low heat until the mixture thickens and doubles in volume, about 10 minutes.

4. In the bowl of a stand mixer fitted with a whisk attachment, add the egg whites and remaining 70 g (⅓ cup) of granulated sugar and whisk until stiff peaks form, about 10 minutes.

5. In a separate bowl, mix the flour and cocoa powder together.

6. Gently pour the chocolate/butter mixture into the whole egg mixture. Fold together carefully so as not to deflate the eggs. Fold in one-third of the meringue. Fold in the flour mixture, then gently fold in the rest of the meringue. Take your time.

7. Pour the batter into the prepared pan and place on a baking sheet. Bake on the center rack for 30 minutes, or until a knife inserted into the center comes out almost clean, with a few crumbs. Remove from the oven and let cool for 30–35 minutes before unmolding onto a serving plate.

For the Marinated Berries

170 g (1 cup) fresh raspberries

100 g (⅔ cup) fresh blueberries

70 g (½ cup) fresh blackberries

9 g (2 teaspoons) vanilla bean paste

50 g (¼ cup) granulated sugar

45 ml (3 tablespoons) water

Chef Tips

Take your time whisking the eggs and the egg whites to ensure the cake will be light and fluffy. If you will be using the same bowl, be sure to wash it well in between. Any leftover fat from the egg yolks—even the smallest amount—can keep the egg whites from whipping up to stiff peaks.

8. To make the mousse: In a small bowl, add in the mascarpone. Whisk it to loosen it. In the bowl of a stand mixer fitted with a whisk attachment, add the mascarpone, heavy cream, powdered sugar, and vanilla bean seeds. Whisk until stiff peak form, about 3 minutes. Load the mousse into the prepared piping bag and pipe rosettes around the perimeter of the cake or simply spread it with an offset spatula. The cream can be stored in a bowl covered with plastic wrap or in a piping bag for up to 2 days in the refrigerator.

9. To make the marinated berries: In a 2- or 3-qt (1.8- or 2.7-l) saucepan, add all of the ingredients. Cover and cook over medium heat, stirring occasionally, until thickened, 15–20 minutes. Chill in the refrigerator for 30 minutes. The berries can be stored in an airtight container in the refrigerator for up to 5 days.

10. To serve, slice the cake and add a dollop of the mascarpone mousse on the side or over the top. Add a spoonful of marinated berries for a nice tart and texture balance. The cake can be stored in an airtight container in the refrigerator for up to 3 days.

Coffee Break Coffee Cake

Coffee break is a very important part of the day, am I right? I wanted to create the perfect crumb cake to go with it. This cake is just firm enough to stand on its own, but soft enough to have the perfect cakey texture. The crunchy cinnamon topping over the soft fluffy cake-like texture makes for the perfect bite, elevating this to the best coffee cake you can make. As a bonus, it also comes together very quickly.

Yield: 4 mini loaf cakes

Prep Time: 20 minutes

Bake Time: 20–25 minutes

Difficulty: Easy

Tools: Rubber spatula, stand mixer, 4 small loaf pans (200 g [7 oz] each), piping bag

For the Cake

113 g (½ cup) unsalted butter, at room temperature

60 g (¼ cup) vegetable oil

100 g (½ cup) granulated sugar

100 g (½ cup) light brown sugar

3 g (1 teaspoon) ground cinnamon

150 g (3) eggs, at room temperature

300 g (2½ cups) all-purpose flour

15 g (1 tablespoon) baking soda

8 g (1½ teaspoons) baking powder

300 g (1¼ cups) sour cream or crème fraîche

For the Topping

113 g (½ cup) unsalted butter, at room temperature

100 g (½ cup) dark brown sugar

50 g (¼ cup) granulated sugar

150 g (1¼ cups) all-purpose flour

1. Preheat the oven to 350°F (175°C). Brush four 200-g (7-oz) loaf pans with butter and line the bottoms and edges with parchment paper.

2. To make the cake: In the bowl of a stand mixer fitted with a paddle attachment, add the butter, oil, granulated sugar, brown sugar, and cinnamon. Whip on medium speed for 5 minutes. Scrape down the sides of the bowl and whip for 5 minutes longer. Add the eggs one at a time, mixing for 2–3 minutes in between each addition.

3. In a separate bowl, add the flour, baking soda, and baking powder. Whisk to combine. Add the dry ingredients to the butter mixture all at once. Mix on low speed to absorb the flour, just for 2 minutes. The batter will be thick. Add the sour cream and mix until the batter is smooth and fluffy.

4. Using a piping bag, pipe the batter into the pans evenly. You can place each pan on a kitchen scale to make sure they weigh the same amount, ensuring they will bake at the same time.

5. To make the topping: In a small bowl, combine all of the ingredients to form the topping. Break into smaller and larger pieces. Spread it out evenly on top of each cake.

6. Bake for 20–25 minutes, or until a toothpick inserted into the center comes out clean.

7. Store the cakes covered with plastic wrap at room temperature for up to 1 week.

Chef Tips
If you pipe the cake batter into the cake pans you will get more height on your cakes.

Funfetti Explosion Cake and Cookies

I cannot wait for you to be as obsessed with this cookie cake as I am. It is so fun and whimsical to make. Chewy cookies and vanilla buttercream hide a sprinkle explosion in the center. There is no waiting on cake layers to cool because we are stacking cookies, so this dessert comes together quickly. Don't tell the kiddos about the hidden sprinkles, and let them be surprised when you cut into the cookie cake.

Yield: 1 mini explosion cake and 10 cookies (35 g [1.25 oz] each)

Prep Time: 1½ hours

Bake Time: 25–35 minutes

Difficulty: Easy

Tools: Silicone mats, stand mixer, rubber spatula, 1-inch (2.5-cm) cookie cutter, piping bag, star tip

For the Cookies

170 g (¾ cup) unsalted butter, at room temperature

100 g (½ cup) granulated sugar

150 g (¾ cup) firmly packed light brown sugar

50 g (1) egg, at room temperature

20 g (1) egg yolk, at room temperature

240 g (2 cups) all-purpose flour

30 g (4 tablespoons) cornstarch

10 g (2 teaspoons) baking powder

50 g (⅓ cup) sprinkles

For the Frosting and Decorations

1 batch American Buttercream (page 46)

80 g (½ cup) sprinkles

1. Preheat the oven to 350°F (175°C). Line two baking sheets with silicone mats or parchment paper.

2. To make the cookies: In the bowl of a stand mixer fitted with a paddle attachment, add the butter, granulated sugar, and brown sugar. Whip on medium speed until fluffy, about 5 minutes. Scrape down the sides of the bowl, add the egg, and whip for 2 minutes. Add the egg yolk and whip for 2 minutes longer, until smooth and fluffy.

3. In a separate bowl, add the flour, cornstarch, and baking powder. Whisk to combine. Add to the butter mixture and mix on low speed just until a dough forms. Do not overmix or the dough will become sticky. Add the 50 g (⅓ cup) of sprinkles and mix for 20 seconds to combine.

4. Weigh out ten 35-g (1¼-oz) cookies and roll them each into a perfect ball, and place on one of the prepared baking sheets; scatter them so they are not in a row. Divide the remaining dough into six equal portions, roll into balls, and place on the second prepared baking sheet.

5. Place the baking sheet with the larger cookies on the center rack of the oven. Bake for 15–20 minutes, until the tops of the cookies are very light golden and the edges are darker golden brown. Remove from the oven and let cool for 10 minutes. Using a 1-inch (2.5-cm) cookie cutter or the bottom of your piping tip, cut out the center of each cookie and set aside. Let the cookies cool to room temperature.

6. Bake the smaller cookies for 10–15 minutes, until lightly golden brown. Remove from the oven and let cool.

7. Transfer the buttercream to a piping bag fitted with a star tip. You will use half of the frosting to build the cookie cake and serve the other half as dip with the smaller cookies.

8. On a cake board or cake stand, pipe a small amount of buttercream and place a large cookie on top; this will be the "glue" for the cake. Pipe a thin layer of frosting around the perimeter of the cookie and stack another one on top. Make sure the holes of the cookies match up in the center. Repeat until you have used five of the large cookies. Fill the center of the cookie cake with most of the 80 g (½ cup) of sprinkles. Top with one of the little cookie cutouts to seal and keep the sprinkles secure. Pipe a thin layer around the perimeter of the top cookie and place the remaining large cookie on top upside down so the flat edge is on the top. Pipe decorations with the frosting and top with a few more sprinkles.

9. Pipe the remaining frosting into a bowl and serve with the smaller cookies alongside the cookie cake.

10. The cookies can be stored at room temperature for up to 3 days. Reserve the cake in the refrigerator until ready to serve. It can be stored in the refrigerator for up to 3 days.

Variations
Add 10 g (1 tablespoon) of cocoa powder and 15 ml (1 tablespoon) of milk to the buttercream to make chocolate frosting.

Chocolate Mousse Express
(Mousse au Chocolat)

This is the dessert I ate the most growing up in Paris, and I can't make it without thinking of my dad, who is the chocoholic of the family. It is a simple preparation, but perfecting it takes real practice. You may be surprised that there are raw eggs in this recipe. Use fresh eggs, and you have nothing to worry about. The egg yolks add a depth of flavor and creamy consistency that makes this dessert somewhere between a mousse and a *pot de crème*. Serve with some fresh berries or whipped cream for added indulgence and serve nice and cold. Using a high-quality dark chocolate is essential to this recipe for the best results.

Yield: 4 servings

Prep Time: 15 minutes

Chill Time: 1 hour minimum

Difficulty: Easy

Tools: Stand mixer, piping bag, rubber spatula

---

150 g (1 cup) 60 percent or 70 percent dark chocolate chips

60 g (4 tablespoons) unsalted butter, at room temperature

300 g (6) eggs, at room temperature, separated

30 g (2 tablespoons) granulated sugar

1. In a microwave-safe bowl or over a bain-marie (double boiler), add the chocolate and butter and heat in 20-second increments, stirring in between each interval, until melted and smooth. Let cool to room temperature.

2. Add the egg yolks to the chocolate butter mixture one at a time and whisk in between each addition. Take care that the chocolate is not hot, otherwise, it will cook the yolks.

3. In the bowl of a stand mixer fitted with a whisk attachment, add the egg whites (be careful to not get ANY of the yolks in there) and sugar and whisk on medium speed until stiff peaks form, about 10 minutes if working with egg whites at room temperature.

4. Add one-third of the egg white mixture to the chocolate mixture and whisk to combine. Add the remaining two-thirds egg whites and gently fold into the chocolate mixture until smooth and no visible whites remain.

5. Transfer to a piping bag without a piping tip and pipe into serving glasses. Chill in the refrigerator for 1 hour minimum.

6. Store in the refrigerator for up to 2 days. The colder and longer these desserts sit, the creamier and fluffier they get.

Variations
Add a shot (40 ml or 2 tablespoons) of cooled espresso, Kahlúa, or Baileys Irish Cream to the chocolate mixture before folding in the meringue.

Chocolate Soufflés

The word *souffler* in French means "to blow." It is from this word that the dessert gets its name. The tricky part about this beautiful dessert is that it only stands tall right out of the oven; a few minutes later and it will sink back down, so be sure to serve it warm, and quickly. You can prepare the batter in advance and whip the egg whites at the last minute to fold them in right before baking. With my recipe, you will be a French pastry chef in no time.

Yield: 6 servings

Prep Time: 20 minutes

Bake Time: 15–20 minutes

Difficulty: Intermediate

Tools: Ramekins, balloon whisk, stand mixer, rubber spatula, piping bag, piping tip, sifter

80 g (⅓ cup) granulated sugar, plus more for dusting

220 ml (1 cup) whole milk

100 ml (⅓ cup) heavy cream

20 g (3 tablespoons) cornstarch

300 g (2 cups) dark chocolate chips

60 g (3) egg yolks, at room temperature

150 g (5) egg whites, at room temperature

Powdered sugar, for dusting, or 1 batch Crème Anglaise (page 42), for serving

Chef Tips

Take your time whipping the egg whites—this step is the key to the success of this recipe.

1. Preheat the oven to 350°F (175°C). Generously brush six 224-g (8-oz) ramekins with butter. Dust each one with a little granulated sugar and tap out any excess.

2. In a 3-qt (2.7-l) saucepan, add the milk, heavy cream, and cornstarch. Whisk together over low heat for 5–6 minutes, until the mixture comes to a boil and thickens.

3. Pour the chocolate chips into a large bowl. Pour the hot milk mixture over the chocolate chips and mix together until smooth.

4. Add the egg yolks one at time, whisking in between each addition to keep the batter very smooth.

5. In the bowl of a stand mixer fitted with a whisk attachment, add the egg whites and granulated sugar and whisk until stiff peaks form, 8–10 minutes. Work with room temperature egg whites for the best meringue.

6. Add one-third of the egg white mixture to the chocolate mixture and whisk to combine. Add the remaining two-thirds of the egg whites and gently fold with a rubber spatula into the chocolate mixture. Be careful not to deflate the egg whites. The volume of these is what makes the soufflés so light and mousse-like.

7. Load the soufflé batter into a piping bag without a piping tip and pipe into each ramekin. Pinch your thumb and index finger together and trace along the edge of the ramekin to make sure the chocolate batter is nice and even and not on the rim. Skipping this step can keep your soufflés from rising properly.

8. Place the ramekins on a baking sheet and bake right away for 15–20 minutes, until the soufflés have risen about 1 inch (2.5 cm) above the edge of the ramekin. Serve immediately, or you know what happens. Dust with a little powdered sugar or serve with crème anglaise.

Edible Cookie Dough Bites

This one is dedicated to my sister, who always insisted on eating the
cookie dough when we made cookies together. I keep these stocked in the freezer
at all times. They are the perfect late-night snack or quick pick-me-up treat.

Yield: 30 pieces of 20 g (¾ oz)
each

Prep Time: 15 minutes

Chill Time: 1 hour

Difficulty: Easy

Tools: Silicone mat, rubber spatula

113 g (½ cup) unsalted butter,
at room temperature

150 g (¾ cup) dark brown sugar

10 ml (2 teaspoons) whole milk,
at room temperature

5 g (1 teaspoon) pure vanilla
extract

128 g (1 cup) heat-treated flour
(see Chef Tips below)

200 g (1¼ cups) mini dark
chocolate chips

Chef Tips

*If you need to "heat treat" your
flour you can simply place it in a
microwave-safe bowl and heat it in
increments of 30 seconds. Mix in
between each time, and check with
a thermometer until you reach a
temperature of 165°F (74°C). Allow
the flour to cool completely before
making your cookie dough or the
dough will be extremely sticky and
melt the chocolate.*

1. Line a baking sheet with a silicone mat or parchment paper.

2. In a mixing bowl, mix together the butter and brown sugar
with a rubber spatula until smooth. Add the milk and vanilla.
Combine with a spatula until the texture is smooth and fully
blended. The butter and sugar should be one color. Add the
flour and mix to combine halfway, then add the mini chocolate
chips and finish mixing. This will keep you from overmixing
the dough.

3. Weigh out pieces of cookie dough on a kitchen scale of 20 g
(¾ oz) each. Roll them into balls and set them on the prepared
baking sheet. Place the sheet in the freezer for 1 hour.

4. Once frozen, place the balls in a large zip-top bag and store
in the freezer for up to 3 weeks, if they last that long.

ABOVE (left to right): Crispy Macadamia Cookies, Edible Cookie Dough Bites

Crispy Macadamia Cookies

Simple but delicious, these crispy buttery macadamia cookies are the perfect addition to any dessert table. They come together quickly and are delicious. They are dear to my heart because they are also my mother's favorite American cookie. For a fun twist, caramelize the macadamia nuts first and achieve an even crunchier texture.

Yield: 20–24 cookies of 60 g (2 oz) each

Prep Time: 15 minutes

Bake Time: 15–20 minutes

Difficulty: Easy

Tools: Silicone mats, stand mixer, rubber spatula

170 g (¾ cup) unsalted butter, at room temperature

100 g (½ cup) granulated sugar

160 g (¾ cup) light brown sugar

50 g (1) egg, at room temperature

20 g (1) egg yolk, at room temperature

270 g (2¼ cups) all-purpose flour

20 g (3 tablespoons) cornstarch

12 g (1 tablespoon) baking powder

120 g (1 cup) unsalted macadamia nuts

120 g (¾ cup) white chocolate chips

1. Preheat the oven 350°F (175°C). Line three or four baking sheets with silicone mats or parchment paper.

2. In the bowl of a stand mixer fitted with a paddle attachment, add the butter, granulated sugar, and brown sugar. Mix for 5 minutes on high speed, until light and creamy. Scrape down the sides of the bowl, add the egg, and mix for 3 minutes longer. Add the egg yolk and mix for 5 minutes longer, until the batter is fluffy and smooth.

3. In a separate bowl, add the flour, cornstarch, and baking powder. Mix to combine. Add to the butter mixture and mix for 2–3 minutes to combine. Fold in the macadamia nuts and white chocolate chips.

4. Roll six cookie dough balls of about 60 g (2 oz) each per baking sheet. Place them on the prepared baking sheets and bake on the center rack for 15 minutes, or until golden brown. The top will be lighter golden brown than around the edges. Remove from the oven and let cool to room temperature.

5. Store in an airtight container at room temperature for up to 4 days. You can store the unbaked cookie dough in the refrigerator for up to 1 week. You can also freeze the unbaked cookie dough balls for baking at a later time. Store them in a zip-top bag for up to 1 month and bake directly from frozen. Simply add 5–7 minutes to the baking time.

Mandel Bread

I have always loved something delicious that's not too sweet and just crunchy enough to enjoy with a warm coffee. If biscotti is usually too hard of a crunch for you, this recipe is your new best friend. These cakelike sticks bake up perfectly and stay crispy, without being overly crunchy. They are just sweet enough to enjoy with your favorite warm beverage. The texture is cakey and crumbly from the oil in the recipe. Using mini chocolate chips is a nice touch, adding some chocolate in every bite.

Yield: 12 large pieces

Prep Time: 10 minutes

Bake Time: 30 minutes

Difficulty: Easy

Tools: Chef's knife, rubber spatula, silicone mat, stand mixer

---

150 g (¾ cup) granulated sugar

215 g (1 cup) vegetable oil, plus more for oiling your hands

150 g (3) eggs, at room temperature

360 g (3 cups) all-purpose flour

15 g (1 tablespoon) baking powder

140 g (1 cup) mini chocolate chips

1. Preheat the oven to 350°F (175°C). Line a baking sheet with a silicone mat or parchment paper.

2. In the bowl of a stand mixer fitted with the paddle attachment, add the sugar, oil, and eggs. Mix for 3–4 minutes, until combined, smooth, and shiny. This dough has a very unique consistency from the oil and it will appear almost stretchy.

3. Add the flour and baking powder and mix just enough to combine; do not overmix or the dough will get very sticky. Add the mini chocolate chips and mix just to combine.

4. Oil your hands and form the dough on the prepared baking sheet into a long flat log about 9 inches (23 cm) long by 6 inches (15 cm) wide, similar to making biscotti.

5. Bake for 20 minutes, or until golden brown all over. Remove from the oven and work quickly using a chef's knife to cut mandel bread at a 40-degree angle, each about 2 inches (5 cm) wide. You should get about twelve pieces total. Leave them on the baking sheet, as they are fragile, and flip them cut-side up.

6. Bake for 5 minutes longer, until lightly golden brown. Flip them to the other side and bake for 5 minutes longer, until lightly golden brown. Transfer to a wire rack and let cool. The final drying minutes are important to create that light, crispy texture and dehydrate the moisture in the dough.

7. Store in an airtight container at room temperature for up to 2 weeks.

Piped Butter Cookies
(Sablés au Beurre)

Everyone needs a quick, easy, and delicious butter cookie in their repertoire. These cookies come together quickly and melt in your mouth. The sable texture is unique and lands between a shortbread and a sugar cookie. Although they are similar to spritz cookies, they are fluffier and less dense. You can flavor the dough with extracts, fresh citrus zest, or honey.

Yield: 20–30 small cookies

Prep Time: 10 minutes

Bake Time: 15–20 minutes

Difficulty: Easy

Tools: Silicone mat, stand mixer, rubber spatula, balloon whisk piping bag, star tip

227 g (1 cup) unsalted butter, at room temperature

80 g (¾ cup) powdered sugar

1 vanilla bean, split and scraped

50 g (1) egg, at room temperature

240 g (2 cups) all-purpose flour

40 g (5 tablespoons) cornstarch

45 ml (3 tablespoons) whole milk, plus more as needed

Chef Tips
Take your time whipping the butter and sugar together to get the mixture nice and fluffy. This will give the cookies a much better consistency and texture.

1. Preheat the oven to 350°F (175°C). Line two or three baking sheets with silicone mats or parchment paper. Fit a piping bag with a star tip and set aside.

2. In the bowl of a stand mixer fitted with a paddle attachment, add the butter, powdered sugar, and vanilla bean seeds. Beat on medium speed for 5–8 minutes, until super fluffy and pale in color. Scrape down the sides of the bowl and add the egg. Beat for 3 minutes longer, until smooth and creamy.

3. In a separate bowl, whisk together the flour and cornstarch. Add to the butter mixture and mix on low speed to combine. Scrape down the sides of the bowl, add the milk, and mix for 2 minutes longer until nice and smooth. If the batter is still a little too thick to pipe, add 15–30 ml (1–2 tablespoons) more milk to loosen it slightly.

4. Load the cookie batter into the prepared piping bag. Pipe rosettes in a circular motion onto the prepared baking sheet. Hold the bag at 90 degrees above the baking sheet, not at an angle. Pipe a little dough in the center, then pipe the rest of the rosette in a counterclockwise motion.

5. Bake one baking sheet at a time on the center rack for 15 minutes. These cookies will stay nice and white when baked, but look for that light golden color along the edges and the bottom of the cookies. Transfer to a wire rack and let cool completely.

6. Store in an airtight container for up to 4 days at room temperature.

Variations
Add lemon zest, orange zest, coffee extract, almond extract, or 2 g (1 teaspoon) of cocoa powder.

Fresh Yogurt Cake
(Gateau Yaourt)

It would be difficult to find a French mom who hasn't made this household staple cake. It is extremely moist and much less dense than a pound cake. Its rich texture is created by the large amount of air whipped into the eggs and the fresh yogurt added to the batter. The yogurt glaze ties the whole cake together with the perfect bite.

Yield: One 9-inch (23-cm) loaf, 8 servings

Prep Time: 20 minutes

Bake Time: 35–40 minutes

Difficulty: Easy

Tools: 9-inch (23-cm) Loaf pan, stand mixer, balloon whisk, offset spatula, paring knife

For the Cake

200 g (4) eggs, at room temperature

200 g (1 cup) granulated sugar

50 g (¼ cup) light brown sugar

75 ml (⅓ cup) grapeseed oil

260 g (1 cup) plain unsweetened yogurt, at room temperature

240 g (2 cups) all-purpose flour

30 g (¼ cup) cornstarch

12 g (2½ teaspoons) baking powder

Zest of 1 orange (optional)

Zest of 1 lemon (optional)

For the Icing

195 g (¾ cup) plain unsweetened yogurt, at room temperature

60 ml (¼ cup) heavy cream, at room temperature

50 g (½ cup) powdered sugar

1. Preheat the oven to 355°F (180°C). Brush a 9 x 4-inch (23 x 10-cm loaf pan with butter and line it with parchment paper.

2. To make the cake: In the bowl of a stand mixer fitted with a whisk attachment, add the eggs, granulated sugar, brown sugar, and oil. Whisk on high speed for 10 full minutes until double in volume, thick, and pale in color. The eggs should be at the ribbon stage (page 22). Reduce the speed to medium, add the yogurt, and mix for 2 minutes, until smooth. There should be no lumps. Make sure the yogurt is at room temperature.

3. In a separate bowl, add the flour, cornstarch, baking powder, and zests (if using). Whisk to combine. In three additions, gently fold into the egg mixture using a rubber spatula, being careful not to deflate the eggs.

4. Pour the batter into the prepared pan and spread evenly using an offset spatula. Place the cake pan on a baking sheet and bake on the center rack for 30 minutes, until a knife inserted into the center comes out clean and the top of the cake is dark golden brown. The outside of this cake will be dark but the inside stays perfectly white. Let the cake sit for 10 minutes before unmolding it, then place it on a cooling rack. Let cool completely.

5. To make the icing: In a bowl, add the yogurt, heavy cream, and powdered sugar and stir until smooth. Spread the icing on the top of the cake using an offset spatula. Serve right away.

6. Wrap the cake in plastic wrap and store in the refrigerator for up to 4 days. Individual slices without icing can be wrapped in plastic wrap and frozen for up to 3 weeks for that perfect morning snack.

Chef Tips
Take your time whipping the eggs, the lightness and moist crumb come from incorporating air into the egg, sugar, and oil mixture.

Citrus Matchstick Cookies

Citrusy, zesty, and full of flavor, these matchstick cookies are so much fun to make and eat. The cookie dough does not spread during baking, allowing you to create these fun shapes that resemble matchsticks. The buttery, shortbread-like consistency is unique, and the white chocolate ganache adds just the right amount of sweetness.

Yield: 18 cookies

Prep Time: 15 minutes

Bake Time: 20–25 minutes

Chill Time: 1 hour

Difficulty: Easy

Tools: Silicone mat, stand mixer, rubber spatula, zester, chef's knife

For the Cookies

227 g (1 cup) unsalted butter, at room temperature

100 g (1 cup) powdered sugar

100 g (½ cup) granulated sugar

1 vanilla bean, split and scraped

100 g (2) eggs, at room temperature

600 g (5 cups) all-purpose flour

Zest and juice of 1 small orange

Zest of 1 lemon

For the White Chocolate Ganache

150 g (1 cup) white chocolate chips

60 ml (¼ cup) heavy cream

Red gel food coloring

Orange gel food coloring

1. Preheat the oven to 350°F (175°C). Line a baking sheet with a silicone mat or parchment paper.

2. To make the cookies: In the bowl of a stand mixer fitted with a paddle attachment, add the butter, powdered sugar, granulated sugar, and vanilla bean seeds. Beat on medium speed for 5–8 minutes, until super fluffy and pale in color. Scrape down the sides of the bowl and add the eggs one at time, mixing for 2 minutes in between each addition.

3. In a separate bowl, add the flour, orange juice and zest, and lemon zest. Add to the butter mixture and mix on low speed to combine. Scrape down the sides of the bowl and mix for 2 minutes longer, until smooth.

4. Place the dough in the center of the prepared baking sheet, lightly wet your hands, and pat the dough into a rectangle about 9 x 6 inches (23 x 15 cm) and 1/2 inch (1.3 cm) thick.

5. Place the baking sheet on the center rack and bake for 20 minutes. Remove from the oven and, with the long side facing you, use a chef's knife to score the dough into sticks about 1 inch (2.5 cm) wide (they will be 6 inches tall). Score the dough again through the middle on the short side, so that you now have 18 cookies. Bake for 5 minutes longer. These cookies will stay a lovely white color when baked. Look for that light golden color along the edges and the bottom of the cookies.

6. Using a chef's knife, work quickly to press down into the scored sticks to separate the cookies. Let cool on a wire rack to room temperature.

7. To make the ganache: In a small microwave-safe bowl, add the white chocolate and heavy cream. Melt for 30 seconds. Stir and heat for 20 seconds longer, until completely melted and smooth.

Chef Tips

Take your time whipping the butter and sugars together to get the mixture nice and fluffy. This will give the cookies a much nicer consistency and texture.

8. Add a small amount of orange food coloring to the bowl and stir to combine. Dip the top half of half of the cookies in the orange ganache. Add 2 drops of red food coloring to the orange and mix to combine. Dip the other half of the cookies into the red ganache. Let cool in the refrigerator for 1 hour, until completely set.

9. Store in an airtight container at room temperature for up to 4 days.

Variations

Add coffee extract, almond extract, or 2 g (1 teaspoon) of cocoa powder for a chocolaty version.

Thick and Chewy Chocolate Chip Cookies

It took me years to create the perfect chocolate chip cookie recipe. I baked hundreds of different ones but they never quite hit the spot like these. These are truly perfection, with a chewy center, delicious crumb, and crispy edges. They are sure to turn any bad day into a good day, and any good day into an even better day. The secret ingredient is cornstarch, which creates the perfect texture and keeps them chewy for days.

Yield: 20 cookies (50 g [1¾ oz]) each

Prep Time: 15 minutes

Bake Time: 12–15 minutes

Difficulty: Easy

Tools: Stand mixer, rubber spatula, silicone mat

170 g (¾ cup) unsalted butter, at room temperature

100 g (½ cup) granulated sugar

160 g (¾ cup) light brown sugar

50 g (1) egg, at room temperature

20 g (1) egg yolk, at room temperature

280 g (2⅓ cups) all-purpose flour

20 g (2½ tablespoons) cornstarch

12 g (2 teaspoons) baking soda

120 g (¾ cup) milk chocolate chips

120 g (¾ cup) dark chocolate chips

1. Preheat the oven to 350°F (175°C) and line two baking sheets with silicone mats or parchment paper.

2. In a stand mixer fitted with a paddle attachment, add the butter, granulated sugar, and brown sugar and mix on medium speed for about 5 minutes. Add the egg and mix for 5 minutes until fully combined. Add the egg yolk and mix for 2 minutes longer until the batter is smooth.

3. In a separate bowl, add the flour, cornstarch, and baking soda. Mix together to combine. Add to the butter mixture and beat until the butter absorbs the flour. Don't overwork the dough; it's fine if there are still some visible streaks of flour.

4. Add the chocolate chips and mix for 2 minutes until the batter is smooth and combined.

5. Divide the dough into even-size balls. A great benchmark is 50 g (1¾ oz) per cookie. Roll them tightly and place on the prepared baking sheets in offset rows.

6. Bake for 12 minutes, or until lightly golden brown. The top of the cookie should still look slightly gooey and soft, with golden edges.

7. Store the baked cookies at room temperature for up to 1 week. You can store any unbaked cookie balls in the freezer in a zip-top bag for up to 1 month. Bake the cookie balls from frozen, adding 3 minutes to the baking time.

Variations

You can substitute the chocolate chips for white chocolate chips and dried cranberries, walnuts, oats, or anything else you like. Make sure you play with the same weight each time. The additions are 240 g (8½ oz), so as long as you add that weight you can make these cookies any flavor you want.

Almond Tuiles
(Tuiles aux Amandes)

One of the most popular cookies among the French petits fours, this crispy, delicate, almond wafer cookie is known for its unique curved shaped and fragile texture. Similarly to meringues, macarons, and ladyfingers, these are all eaten plain right out of the oven. Many other petits fours require much more patience and preparations, like glazes, icings, or fillings, but not the tuile. Almond tuiles made their debut and became popular in the early 1900s and it's common to find them in most patisseries around France today.

Yield: 50 tuiles

Prep Time: 10 minutes

Bake Time: 5–6 minutes

Difficulty: Easy

Tools: Silicone mat, rubber spatula, offset spatula, rolling pin

---

60 g (½ cup) all-purpose flour

230 g (2 cups) powdered sugar

50 g (1) egg, at room temperature

150 g (5) egg whites, at room temperature

1 vanilla bean, split and scraped, or 9 g (2 teaspoons) vanilla bean paste

113 g (½ cup) unsalted butter, melted

240 g (3½ cups) sliced untoasted almonds

Chef Tips
Work quickly with the tuiles; as soon as they come out of the oven slide them off the baking mat and onto the rolling pin. You can only do this while they are still warm or they will remain flat. Once cooled, they crack very easily, so handle gently.

1. Preheat the oven to 350°F (175°C). Line a very flat baking sheet with a silicone mat or parchment paper.

2. In a mixing bowl with a wooden spoon or rubber spatula, add the flour and powdered sugar. Mix to combine. As you mix, add the egg and egg whites a little a time, mixing in between each addition to get a smooth batter. This is crucial to make these delicate wafers: the batter must be completely smooth. Add the vanilla bean seeds and mix gently to combine.

3. Stream the butter into the batter as you mix it together. The batter should be completely smooth. Lastly, add the sliced almonds and stir to combine.

4. Spoon a teaspoon of the batter onto the prepared baking sheet, smoothing it flat with the back of a spoon. Bake no more than five tuiles at once so you have the time to remove them all and place them on a rolling pin to achieve the perfect shape.

5. Place on the center rack, baking one sheet at a time, and bake for 5–6 minutes, until the edges are golden brown. The center will stay fairly white.

6. Slide the tuiles off the baking sheet one a time using an offset spatula and place on a rolling pin so that they curve into the classic shape. Let cool completely.

7. Store in an airtight container at room temperature for up to 3 days.

Let's Get Technical

From troubleshooting to baking terms,
here's everything you need to know.

Baking Troubleshooting

Most mistakes in baking can be avoided by reading through the full recipe before you begin baking. Measure out every ingredient and prepare the baking sheets or pans ahead of time.

Below are a few quick fixes to some of the common issues you may face in baking.

THE CENTER OF THE CAKE COLLAPSED

Chances are it is just underbaked or you interrupted the baking process by opening the oven. This is fixable if you act quickly. Though the result won't be perfect, you can reheat the oven to a slightly higher temperature and place the cake back in to finish baking. If the cake is already dark or nice and golden, simply cover it with aluminum foil before placing it in the oven.

THE PIE CRUST DOUGH IS TOO STRETCHY

It's happened to us all: when we reroll pie crust we notice the dough gets stretchy and difficult to roll out. It retracts onto itself, making it impossible to get a perfectly rolled-out dough. But we can fix it. Simply squeeze a small amount of lemon juice onto the dough, roll it back into a flat disk shape, and place in the refrigerator for a few hours. The gluten will have time to relax and the dough will be as good as new.

THE BUTTERCREAM IS SOUPY

Chances are the butter just got too warm. Making sure the butter is soft and spreadable before you start is very important to get that beautiful fluffy consistency. Think of this as the one recipe you can't overwhip or overmix. If the buttercream is looking a little soupy, simply put it in the refrigerator for 15 minutes, then place it back on the mixer and mix for 10 minutes on medium speed. Repeat this step several times until the desired consistency is obtained.

THE BATTER IS TOO STIFF

Baking can be affected by many things, including the weather and high altitude. Sometimes the batter will appear a little stiff. If you are baking cake layers in increments and the batter sits in the bowl it can also become stiff and change the final crumb of the cake. To loosen the batter, add 30 ml (2 tablespoons) of milk, cream, or half-and-half to smooth it out. This will not denature the recipe and will keep the batter perfect as you continue to bake in batches.

Baking Terms

Aged egg whites The process of keeping separated egg whites from fresh eggs in a container in the refrigerator. These are very important when making things such as macarons. They will begin to liquefy, which makes for larger and much fluffier meringues.

Bain-marie A double boiler. This tool is very useful when heating different preparations in baking or chocolate tempering. The water adds a barrier to keep ingredients from burning or overcooking. You still always want to stand by the bain-marie to keep an eye on it because it can get very hot quickly.

Bench proof This is generally the first proofing that occurs for bread. To do this, simply place the dough in an oiled bowl and set it in a warm, dark place for ideal growth. This process happens before shaping and proofing one last time before baking.

Beurre pommade One degree past soft butter. At this consistency, the butter should be completely spreadable and resemble the texture of hand lotion. This is the texture you obtain before butter is melted.

Blind baking The process of baking a dough for a tart or dessert before adding the filling to it. This is common for desserts like lemon meringue tarts, where the filling does not need to be baked.

Chemical leavening Refers to ingredients such as baking soda or baking powder that are used to make a batter rise.

Docking A fancy way of saying prick the dough to create small holes. Docking produces an even rise in the oven and also allows steam to escape the dough properly without causing too many imperfections in the final product.

Double fold or single fold This technique is used for puff pastry. See the diagram on page 33.

Mechanical leavening The result of incorporating air into a batter to create a delicate texture.

Mise en place Literally means to put into its place.

Organic leavening A method of leavening achieved through fermentation. In this process, yeast is used to produce carbon dioxide which causes the product to rise.

Panade Refers to the dough you make during the pâte à choux process by quickly beating the flour into the milk and butter. This dough then needs to be properly cooked and dehydrated before it is then rehydrated with eggs.

Paton A French baking term referring to the storing of different doughs. Create a bricklike flat shape with the dough and wrap it in plastic wrap, then place in the refrigerator and chill for 1 hour. This also refers to the pastry being ready for future use.

Petits fours Literally translated means "little oven." To count as petits fours, the baked item should be two or three bites at the most. These are intended to be elegant small bites to share after a meal. Most of them require several preparations to complete, such as mini éclairs, mini choux, macarons, or mini tartelettes. They are sophisticated and offer a wide range of textures and flavors.

Soft butter When a recipe calls for soft butter it implies room-temperature butter. When specified in a recipe, this is essential to the success of that recipe to allow ingredients to incorporate together correctly for the desired texture. Soft butter should be completely spreadable.

CONVERSION CHARTS

DRY INGREDIENTS

	1 tsp	1 tbsp	¼ cup	⅓ cup	½ cup	⅔ cup	¾ cup	1 cup
Baking Powder	4 g	14 g	56 g (2 oz)	75 g (2.7 oz)	112 g (4 oz)	150 g (5.3 oz)	168 g (6 oz)	224 g (8 oz)
Baking Soda	5 g	17 g	68 g (2.4 oz)	90 g (3 oz)	136 g (5 oz)	180 g (6 oz)	204 g (7 oz)	272 g (9.5 oz)
Chocolate Chips	2.5 g	7.5 g	30 g (0.6 oz)	40 g (1.2 oz)	60 g (1.3 oz)	80 g (2.4 oz)	90 g (2.6 oz)	120 g (3.5 oz)
Cocoa Powder	2 g	6 g	25 g (0.9 oz)	33 g (1.2 oz)	50 g (1.3 oz)	66 g (2.4 oz)	75 g (2.6 oz)	100 g (3.5 oz)
Cornstarch	3 g	10 g	40 g (1.4 oz)	53 g (1.9 g)	80 g (2.8 g)	106 g (3.7 oz)	120 g (4.2 oz)	160 g (5.6 oz)
Flour (All-Purpose, Bread, and Cake)	2.5 g	7.5 g	30 g (0.6 oz)	40 g (1.2 oz)	60 g (1.3 oz)	80 g (2.4 oz)	90 g (2.6 oz)	120 g (3.5 oz)
Flour, Nut	2 g	6 g	25 g (0.9 oz)	33 g (1.2 oz)	50 g (1.3 oz)	66 g (2.4 oz)	75 g (2.6 oz)	100 g (3.5 oz)
Sugar, Brown (Light and Dark)	4 g	12 g	50 g (1.75 oz)	66 g (2.3 oz)	100 g (3.5 oz)	132 g (4.7 oz)	150 g (5.3 oz)	200 g (7 oz)
Sugar, Granulated	4 g	12 g	50 g (1.75 oz)	66 g (2.3 oz)	100 g (3.5 oz)	132 g (4.7 oz)	150 g (5.3 oz)	200 g (7 oz)
Sugar, Powdered	2.5 g	7.5 g	30 g (0.6 oz)	40 g (1.2 oz)	60 g (1.3 oz)	80 g (2.4 oz)	90 g (2.6 oz)	120 g (3.5 oz)

LIQUIDS

	1 tsp (5 ml)	1 tbsp (15 ml)	¼ cup (59 ml)	⅓ cup (78 ml)	½ cup (118 ml)	⅔ cup (156 ml)	¾ cup (177 ml)	1 cup (236 ml)
Butter, melted	5 g	15 g	60 g	80 g	120 g	160 g	180 g	240 g
Heavy Cream	5 g	15 g	60 g	80 g	120 g	160 g	180 g	240 g
Milk	5 g	15 g	60 g	80 g	120 g	160 g	180 g	240 g
Oil	4 g	14 g	56 g	75 g	112.5 g	150 g	169 g	225 g
Water	5 g	15 g	59 g	78 g	118 g	156 g	177 g	236 g

SOLIDS

(Butter, Cream Cheese, Shortening, Cheeses)

cup	gram	fl ounce	tablespoon
⅛ cup	28 g	1 oz	2 tbsp
¼ cup	56 g	2 oz	4 tbsp
⅓ cup	75 g	2½ oz	5.3 tbsp
½ cup	112 g	4 oz	8 tbsp
⅔ cup	150 g	5 oz	10.5 tbsp
¾ cup	168	6 oz	12 tbsp
1 cup	225 g	8 oz	16 tbsp

VOLUME MEASUREMENT EQUIVALENTS

cup	fl ounce	tablespoon	teaspoon	milliliter
1 cup	8 oz	16 tbsp	48 tsp	237 ml
¾ cup	6 oz	12 tbsp	36 tsp	177 ml
⅔ cup	5 ⅓ oz	10.6 tbsp	32 tsp	158 ml
½ cup	4 oz	8 tbsp	24 tsp	118 ml
⅓ cup	2 ⅔ oz	5.3 tbsp	16 tsp	79 ml
¼ cup	2 oz	4 tbsp	12 tsp	59 ml
⅛ cup	1 oz	2 tbsp	6 tsp	30 ml
¹⁄₁₆ cup	½ oz	1 tbsp	3 tsp	15 ml

About the Author

Pastry diploma in hand and college degree secured, Chef Mel's professional baking journey began in Paris, where she trained with some of the biggest pastry chef icons, including Pierre Hermé, François Payard, and Laurent Duchêne. She opened a bakery in Paris at the age of twenty-six and created mesmerizing events, bringing the rainbow cake to Paris for the first time with appearances on *Top Chef France*, *M6*, TF1, *100% Mag*, and in hundreds of articles.

Chef Mel went on to create the first-ever edible cupcake dress for the Salon du Chocolat in both Paris and London. She won the Food Network's *Chopped* twice. Chef Mel brings you fifteen years of pastry savoir faire, expert baking kit experiences, and the industry's best-kept secrets. Come meet your butter half, Chef Mel.

Acknowledgments

To my sister: Thank you for the endless brainstormings, creative sessions, and work you have done to help me over the years to make this book a dream come true. The truth is that it would not exist without you.

To Andre Goy: The world's best doctor who brought me back to health and life, allowing me to do what I love every day. Without you I just would not be here.

To Chef Claudia Silva: You were my first chef in culinary school, and you immediately noticed this spark in me and shared your passion for pastry with me; without you I wouldn't be the chef I am today. Thank you for being on this journey with me.

To Heather: You were one of the first investors in Bake it with Mel, and believed in my dream and passion from our very first conversation. Thank you for the opportunity to dream big and help this book become a reality.

To Ian: You have been my best friend, travel partner, and with you I have discovered some of the best restaurants, desserts, and chefs from all over the world. Thanks for being a designated foodie with me.

INDEX

A

active yeast, 12
aged egg whites, 206
alcohol-free wine, 60
Almond Cream
    Frangipane, 50
    Mini Almond Puff Pastry Raspberry Boats, 167
    recipe, 49
almonds
    almandine tarts, 49
    Almond Caramel Topping, 70–1
    Almond Cream, 49, 50
    almond croissant butter, 14
    almond croissants, 49
    Almond Puff Pastry Raspberry Boats, 167
    Almond Tuiles, 202
    Granny's Famous Biscotti, 64–5
    Helenettes, 86
    Krispy Coco Granola, 170
    Mini Almond Puff Pastry Raspberry Boats, 167
    Mocha Cake, 157
    Monsieur Hazelnut Financier, 72–3
    Old Fashioned Macarons, 66
    Pear Almond Galette, 150
    Raspberry Blossom Almond Cake Bites, 76–7
    Rocher topping, 113
    Rum Nantes Cake, 176
    Swiss Rochers, 175
American buttercream
    Funfetti Explosion Cake and Cookies, 184–5
    recipe, 46
apples
    Mini Apple Turnovers, 164
    My Famous Tarte Tatin, 148–9

B

bain-marie, 24, 26, 206
baking basics
    avoiding substitutions, 19
    baking scale, 18
    equipment, 17, 18–19
    glossary of terms, 206–7
    ingredients, 12–15, 18, 19, 26
    pans, 17, 18, 19
    stand mixer, 19, 22
    timers, 18–19
    tips and tricks, 18–19
    tools, 16, 18–19
    troubleshooting, 206
baking pans
    buttering, 23
    choosing, 17, 18, 19
baking powder, 13, 208
baking scale, 18
baking sheets, 19
baking soda, 13, 208
baking techniques
    bread dough, 19, 25
    buttering pans, 23
    chocolate-based batters, 23
    cream butter method, 22, 32, 36
    dusting fruit with cornstarch, 26
    dusting with powdered sugar, 34

egg wash, 35, 36, 38, 39, 82, 119, 125, 133, 137,
    158, 161, 164, 166, 167
meringues, 24–5
mixing, 19, 22
overmixing, 19, 22, 37, 129
puff pastry, 23, 33–4
room-temperature ingredients, 12, 18, 23, 24,
    25, 30, 39, 45, 55, 66, 115, 127, 129
scraping vanilla beans, 60
tempering chocolate, 26
tempering egg yolk mixture, 42, 43, 44
tips for perfect cookies, 23
using ice water, 34, 37
whipping egg whites, 12, 26, 30, 59, 127, 181
whipping egg yolks, 59, 127
Basic Brown Sugar Cookie Dough, 41
Basic Soft and Chewy Sugar Cookies, 40
Basque Cake, 118–19
beignets, 144–5
berries
    French Strawberry Shortcake, 141
    Raspberry Blossom Almond Cake Bites, 76–7
    Raspberry Charlotte, 142, 144
    Raspberry Cinnamon Nonnettes, 85
    Rich and Fluffy Chocolate Cake with Magic
        Mascarpone Mousse and Marinated
        Berries, 180–1
beurre pommade, 18, 207
Birthday Sheet Cake, 115
biscotti, 64–5
bread
    bench proof, 206–7
    French Brioche Dough, 35
bread dough
    baking techniques, 19, 25
    windowpane test, 25
breakfast foods
    breakfast pastries, 33
    Giant Frosted Choco Tart, 158
    Krispy Coco Granola, 170
    Mini Cookie Cereal, 103
    Waffle Sticks with Maple Butter, 104
brioche cake, 133
brioche dough
    recipe, 35
    Tropézienne Tart, 133
brown butter, 72, 73
brown sugar
    about, 14
    Basic Brown Sugar Cookie Dough, 41
    conversion chart, 208
brownies, 120
butter
    almond croissant butter, 14
    beurre pommade, 18, 207
    brown butter, 72, 73
    buttering pans, 23
    conversion chart, 208
    European-style butter, 12, 19, 41
    making, 15
    maple butter, 104
    melted, 208
    salted vs. unsalted, 26
    soft butter, 207
    storing, 15

temperature of, 12, 18, 45, 115
    Thick Salted Butter Caramel Sauce, 58
    vanilla butter, 14
    whipped butters, 14
    whole egg foam batter, 22
butter cookies
    Piped Butter Cookies, 194
buttercream
    about, 24, 46
    American buttercream, 46
    buttercream frosting, 157
    common problems, 206
    French buttercream, 45
    French *Pâte à Bomb* Buttercream, 48
    Funfetti Explosion Cake and Cookies, 184–5
    restoring if broken, 46
    Swiss Meringue Buttercream, 47
    troubleshooting, 206
buttermilk, 15

C

cake flour, 14
cakes
    Basque Cake, 118–19
    Birthday Sheet Cake, 115
    brioche cake, 133
    buttercream for, 45–8
    Chocolate Party Pavlova, 134–5
    Citrus Sunset Cake with Honey Glaze, 116–17
    Coffee Break Coffee Cake, 183
    common problems, 206
    French Strawberry Shortcake, 141
    Fresh Yogurt Cake, 197
    Funfetti Explosion Cake and Cookies, 184–5
    Genoise, 30, 157
    Golden Rocher Pound Cake, 112–13
    Hazelnut Dacquoise Cake, 31
    Japanese-Inspired Cheesecake, 128–9
    Mille Crêpes cake, 130
    Mini Cake Popsicles, 179
    Mocha Cake, 157
    Paris-Brest to Share, 45, 124–5
    pavlova, 134–5
    pound cake, 112–13
    Raspberry Cinnamon Nonnettes, 85
    Rich and Fluffy Chocolate Cake with Magic
        Mascarpone Mousse and Marinated
        Berries, 180–1
    Rum Nantes Cake, 176
    sheet cake, 115
    simple syrup for, 61, 134, 135
    Soft as Cotton Cheesecake, 128–9
    strawberry shortcake, 141
    Swiss Roll, 126–7
    Tropézienne Tart, 133
    troubleshooting, 206
caramel
    about, 57
    Almond Caramel Topping, 70–1
    Citrus Sunset Cake with Honey Glaze, 116–17
    Dry Caramel, 57
    Hazelnut Praline Paste, 53
    My Famous Tarte Tatin, 148–9
    Salted Butter Caramel Popcorn, 171

Thick Salted Butter Caramel Sauce, 58
Wet Caramel, 57
Cat's Tongue Cookies, 99
charlotte, Raspberry Charlotte, 142, 144
cheese
    Japanese-Inspired Cheesecake, 128–9
    Rich and Fluffy Chocolate Cake with Magic
        Mascarpone Mousse and Marinated
        Berries, 180–1
    Soft as Cotton Cheesecake, 128–9
chocolate
    baking techniques for chocolate cake, 23
    baking with, 13, 19
    brownies, 120
    Chocolate Bark, 174
    Chocolate Fondant Cake Bites, 81
    Chocolate Ganache, 54, 107, 134–5, 137
    Chocolate Mousse Express, 187
    Chocolate Party Pavlova, 134–5
    chocolate pastry cream, 44
    Chocolate Salami, 90
    Chocolate Soufflés, 188
    Creamy Chocolate Truffles, 173
    Dark Chocolate Bark, 174
    Delicate Sandwich Cookies, 107
    Edible Cookie Dough Bites, 190
    Elegant Chocolate Éclairs, 137
    Fudgy Brownie Cookies, 68–9
    Giant Frosted Choco Tart, 158
    Homemade Hazelnut Chocolate Spread, 52
    Mandel Bread, 193
    melting, 168
    Mini Cake Popsicles, 179
    Mini Palmier Hearts, 96–7
    Mocha Cake, 157
    Pantry Chocolaty Snack Mix, 168
    pavlova, 134–5
    Raspberry Charlotte, 142, 144
    Rich and Fluffy Chocolate Cake with Magic
        Mascarpone Mousse and Marinated
        Berries, 180–1
    Smores Cookie Pizza, 138
    Soft as Cotton Cheesecake, 129
    Swiss Rochers, 175
    tempering, 26
    Thick and Chewy Chocolate Chip Cookies,
        201
    "three Ss," 26
    in whipped cream, 127, 130
chocolate chips
    Basic Brown Sugar Cookie Dough, 41
    Chocolate Fondant Cake Bites, 81
    Chocolate Mousse Express, 187
    Chocolate Party Pavlova, 134–5
    Chocolate Salami, 90
    Chocolate Soufflés, 188
    Coconut Scone Brunch Bites, 78
    conversion chart, 208
    Creamy Chocolate Truffles, 173
    Crispy Oatmeal Milk Chocolate Chip
        Cookies, 67
    Dark Chocolate Bark, 174
    Edible Cookie Dough Bites, 190
    Fudgy Brownie Cookies, 68–9
    Mandel Bread, 193
    Mini Cake Popsicles, 179
    Mini Cookie Cereal, 103
    Mocha Cake, 157
    Smores Cookie Pizza, 138
    Thick and Chewy Chocolate Chip Cookies,
        201

Chouquettes Chérie, 82
choux puffs
    Lemon Meringue Choux, 100
    Pâte à Choux Dough, 29, 38–9, 82
    XL Fresh Strawberry Choux to Share, 161
    See also Pâte à Choux
Chuffins, 93
Churro Bites, 147
cinnamon
    Pillowy Soft Cinnamon Sugar Pretzels, 122–3
    spiced syrup, 61
Citrus Matchstick Cookies, 198–9
Citrus Sunset Cake with Honey Glaze, 116–17
coconut
    Coconut Scone Brunch Bites, 78
    Krispy Coco Granola, 170
coffee
    Coffee Break Coffee Cake, 183
    Mocha Cake, 157
cookies
    Almond Tuiles, 202
    baking techniques for cookie dough, 19
    baking time, 23
    Basic Brown Sugar Cookie Dough, 41
    Basic Soft and Chewy Sugar Cookies, 40
    Cat's Tongue Cookies, 90, 99
    Citrus Matchstick Cookies, 198–9
    Crispy Macadamia Cookies, 191
    Crispy Oatmeal Milk Chocolate Chip
        Cookies, 67
    Delicate Sandwich Cookies, 107
    Diamond Cookies, 89
    Edible Cookie Dough Bites, 190
    Florentine Bars, 70–1
    Fudgy Brownie Cookies, 68–9
    Funfetti Explosion Cake and Cookies, 184–5
    Helenettes, 86
    Madame Madeleine, 75
    Mini Cookie Cereal, 103
    Old-Fashioned Macarons, 66
    Piped Butter Cookies, 194
    resting the dough, 19, 23
    Smores Cookie Pizza, 138
    Thick and Chewy Chocolate Chip Cookies,
        201
    tips for perfect cookies, 23
craquelin dough, 38, 39, 100
cream butter method, 22, 32, 36
Creamy Chocolate Truffles, 173
Crème Anglaise
    for ice cream base, 43
    for sauce, 42
crème fraiche, 15, 78, 183
Crème Légère, 45
Crème Mousseline
    French Strawberry Shortcake, 141
    Paris-Brest to Share, 45, 125
    recipe, 45
crepes
    Mille Crêpes cake, 130
    Pretty Buttery Crepes, 55
    savory, 55
Crispy Macadamia Cookies, 191
Crispy Oatmeal Milk Chocolate Chip Cookies, 67
crumb cake, Coffee Break Coffee Cake, 183
custards and creams
    Almond Cream, 49
    American buttercream, 46
    Basque Cake, 118–19
    Crème Légère, 45
    Crème Mousseline, 45, 125

diplomat cream, 45
Frangipane, 50
French buttercream, 45
French *Pâte à Bomb* Buttercream, 48
Pastry Cream, 44
Swiss Meringue Buttercream, 47
whipped cream, 126–7
whipped cream filling, 130

D

dairy ingredients, 12, 14, 208
dark brown sugar, 14
Delicate Sandwich Cookies, 107
desserts
    '90s Brownies, 120
    about, 63, 163
    Chocolate Mousse Express, 187
    Chocolate Pudding Cups, 108
    Chocolate Salami, 90
    Chocolate Soufflés, 188
    Chuffins, 93
    Churro Bites, 147
    Creamy Chocolate Truffles, 173
    Dark Chocolate Bark, 174
    Elegant Chocolate Éclairs, 137
    Florentine Bars, 70–1
    French Beignets, 144–5
    Fresh Strawberry Tart, 153
    Granny's Famous Biscotti, 64–5
    Helenettes, 86
    Homemade Ladyfingers, 59
    Madame Madeleine, 75
    Mandel Bread, 193
    Mini Almond Puff Pastry Raspberry Boats, 167
    Mini Apple Turnovers, 164
    Monsieur Hazelnut Financier, 72–3
    Pantry Chocolaty Snack Mix, 168
    Pillowy Soft Cinnamon Sugar Pretzels, 122–3
    poaching liquid for stone fruits, 60
    Raspberry Blossom Almond Cake Bites, 76–7
    Raspberry Charlotte, 142, 144
    Raspberry cinnamon Nonnettes, 85
    Smores Cookie Pizza, 138
    Swiss Rochers, 175
    Waffle Sticks with Maple Butter, 104
    XL Fresh Strawberry Choux to Share, 161
    XL Queen of Hearts, 154
    See also bite-size delicacies; cookies; quick
        treats
Diamond Cookies, 89
dough
    about, 101
    blind baking, 207
    common problems, 206
    docking, 207
    Edible Cookie Dough Bites, 190
    elasticity of, 25
    fixing sticky dough, 34, 37
    gluten development in, 25, 55
    mixing and overmixing, 19, 22, 37
    resting, 19, 23
    sable dough, 32, 36, 70
    storing cookie dough, 40
    troubleshooting, 206
    windowpane test, 25
    See also batter; dough recipes
dough recipes
    Basic Brown Sugar Cookie Dough, 41
    Basic Soft and Chewy Sugar Cookies, 40
    Easy Flaky Crust, 36, 158

French Brioche Dough, 35
Pâte à Choux Dough, 29, 38–9, 82
Quiche Dough, 37
Rough Puff Pastry, 33–4, 154, 164, 167
sable dough, 32, 36, 70
Sweet Pastry Dough, 32
Dry Caramel, 57
dry yeast, 12

E

Easy Flaky Crust
    Giant Frosted Choco Tart, 158
    recipe, 36
éclairs, *Pâte à Choux* Dough, 29, 38–9, 82
Edible Cookie Dough Bites, 190
egg wash, 35, 36, 38, 39, 82, 119, 125, 133, 137, 158, 161, 164, 166, 167
egg whites
    folding, 25
    Krispy Coco Granola, 170
    ladyfingers, 59
    meringue baking techniques, 24–5, 94
    separating eggs, 25
    Swiss Meringue Buttercream, 47
    whipping, 12, 26, 30, 59, 127, 181
egg yolks
    tempering, 42, 43, 44
    whipping, 59, 127
eggs
    aged egg whites, 206
    egg wash, 35, 36, 38, 39, 82, 119, 125, 133, 137, 158, 161, 164, 166, 167
    fresh eggs vs. carton eggs, 12, 26
    raw, in Chocolate Mousse Express, 187
    ribbon stage, 22
    at room temperature, 12, 18, 23, 24, 25, 30, 39, 66, 115, 127, 129
    separating, 25
    temperature of, 66
    tempering egg yolk mixture, 42, 43, 44
    using proper amount of, 12
    whole egg foam batter, 22
    See also egg wash; egg whites; egg yolks
Elegant Chocolate Éclairs, 137
European-style butter, 12, 19, 41

F

fillings
    Almond Paste, 49
    Basque Cake, 118–19
    Chocolate Ganache, 54, 107, 134–5
    Frangipane, 50
    Hazelnut Praline Paste, 53
    Marzipan, 51
    Swiss Roll, 126–7
    whipped cream filling, 130
    See also buttercream; custards and creams; pastes; spreads
financier, *Monsieur Hazelnut Financier*, 72–3
Florentine Bars, 70–1
flourless chocolate cake
    baking techniques, 23
    batter, 22
fluid ounces, measurement equivalents, 209
folding egg whites, 25
fondant, Chocolate Fondant Cake Bites, 81
French Beignets, 144–5
French Brioche Dough, 35
French buttercream, 45

French meringue, 24, 56
French pastry
    about, 29
    baking basics. *See* baking basics
    baking techniques. *See* baking techniques
    recipes. *See* bite-size delicacies; cakes; celebratory cakes; cookies; custards and creams; fillings; master recipes; pastes; quick treats; spreads
French *Pâte à Bomb* Buttercream, 48
French Strawberry Shortcake, 141
Fresh Strawberry Choux to Share, 161
Fresh Strawberry Tart, 153
Fresh Yogurt Cake, 197
frosting, buttercream frosting, 157
fruit
    Citrus Matchstick Cookies, 198–9
    Citrus Sunset Cake with Honey Glaze, 116–7
    Coconut Scone Brunch Bites, 78
    French Strawberry Shortcake, 141
    Fresh Strawberry Tart, 153
    fresh vs. frozen, 26, 77
    Mini Almond Puff Pastry Raspberry Boats, 167
    Mini Apple Turnovers, 164
    My Famous Tarte Tatin, 148–9
    Pear Almond Galette, 150
    poaching liquid for stone fruits, 60
    Raspberry Blossom Almond Cake Bites, 76–7
    Raspberry Charlotte, 142, 144
    Raspberry Cinnamon Nonnettes, 85
    Rich and Fluffy Chocolate Cake with Magic Mascarpone Mousse and Marinated Berries, 180–1
    topping for Japanese-Inspired Cheesecake, 128–9
    XL Fresh Strawberry Choux to Share, 161
fruit tarts, Sweet Pastry Dough, 32
Fudgy Brownie Cookies, 68–9
Funfetti Explosion Cake and Cookies, 184–5

G

Galettes, Pear Almond Galette, 150
ganache
    Chocolate Party Pavlova, 134–5
    Creamy Chocolate Truffles, 173
    Delicate Sandwich Cookies, 107
    Elegant Chocolate Éclairs, 137
    recipe, 54, 135
    Smores Cookie Pizza, 138
    white chocolate ganache, 54, 198–9
Genoise
    about, 22
    Mocha Cake, 157
    recipe, 30
Giant Frosted Choco Tart, 158
Golden Rocher Pound Cake, 112–13
Granny's Famous Biscotti, 64–5
granola, Krispy Coco Granola, 170
ground nuts. *See* nuts

H

hazelnuts
    Chocolate Salami, 90
    Dark Chocolate Bark, 174
    Hazelnut Dacquoise Cake, 31
    Hazelnut Praline Paste, 53
    Helenettes, 86
    Homemade Hazelnut Chocolate Spread, 52
    Monsieur Hazelnut Financier, 72–3

Swiss Rochers, 175
Helenettes, 86
Homemade Ladyfingers, 59

I

ice cream, *Crème Anglaise* Ice Cream Base, 43
icing, royal icing, 158
inverted sugar, 24, 57
Italian meringue, 24, 94, 100

J

Japanese-Inspired Cheesecake, 128–9

K

Krispy Coco Granola, 170

L

ladyfingers
    batter, 22
    Homemade Ladyfingers recipe, 59
    in Raspberry Charlotte, 142, 144
lemon curd, 199
Lemon Meringue Choux, 100
liquid fat mixing, 22
liquid ingredients, conversion chart, 208, 209

M

macadamia nuts, Crispy Macadamia Cookies, 191
macarons
    meringue for, 24
    Old-Fashioned Macarons, 66
Madame Madeleine, 75
madeleines, 75
Mandel Bread, 193
maple butter, 104
marzipan
    French Strawberry Shortcake, 141
    recipe, 51
mascarpone mousse, Rich and Fluffy Chocolate Cake with Magic Mascarpone Mousse and Marinated Berries, 180–1
meringue
    baking techniques, 24–5, 94
    French meringue, 24, 56
    Italian meringue, 24, 94, 100
    Lemon Meringue Choux, 100
    Meringue Kisses, 94
    overmixing, 129
    Swiss meringue, 24
    Swiss Meringue Buttercream, 47
    tips for making, 24–5, 127
Mille Crêpes cake, 130
milliliters, volume measurement equivalents, 209
Mini Almond Puff Pastry Raspberry Boats, 167
Mini Apple Turnovers, 164
Mini Cake Popsicles, 179
Mini Cookie Cereal, 103
Mini Palmier Hearts, 96–7
Mini Swiss Pastries, 166
Mocha Cake, 157
Monsieur Hazelnut Financier, 72–3
mousse
    Chocolate Mousse Express, 187
    Raspberry Charlotte, 142, 144
    Rich and Fluffy Chocolate Cake with Magic

Mascarpone Mousse and Marinated
Berries, 180–1
My Famous Tarte Tatin, 148–9

N

'90s Brownies, 120
nonnettes, 85
nuts
Almond Cream, 49
Almond Paste, 49
Almond Tuiles, 202
Chocolate Salami, 90
Crispy Macadamia Cookies, 191
Dark Chocolate Bark, 174
Hazelnut Dacquoise Cake, 31
Hazelnut Praline Paste, 53
Helenettes, 86
Homemade Hazelnut Chocolate Spread, 52
Krispy Coco Granola, 170
Marzipan, 51
Mini Almond Puff Pastry Raspberry Boats, 167
Mocha Cake, 157
Monsieur Hazelnut Financier, 72–3
nut flour, 12, 14
Old-Fashioned Macarons, 66
Pear Almond Galette, 150
Rum Nantes Cake, 176
Swiss Rochers, 175

O

Oatmeal Milk Chocolate Chip Cookies, 67
Old-Fashioned Macarons, 66

P

palmiers, 33, 154
panade, 38, 207
pancakes, 56
Pantry Chocolaty Snack Mix, 168
Paris-Brest, 45, 124–5
pastes, Hazelnut Praline Paste, 53
pastry cream
Basque Cake, 118–19
Frangipane, 50
Fresh Strawberry Tart, 153
Mini Swiss Pastries, 166
recipe, 29, 44
vanilla bean pastry cream, 29, 44, 153
Pâte à Choux
about, 29
Chouquettes Chérie, 82
Elegant Chocolate Éclairs, 137
Paris-Brest to Share, 45, 124–5
recipe, 38–9
See also choux puffs
pavlova, 134
pavlovas, meringue for, 24
Pear Almond Galette, 150
pies
Easy Flaky Crust, 36
Quiche Dough, 37
Sweet Pastry Dough, 32
Pillowy Soft Cinnamon Sugar Pretzels, 122–3
Piped Butter Cookies, 194
poaching, poaching liquid for stone fruits, 60
popcorn, Salted Butter Caramel Popcorn, 171
pound cake, 112–13
Pretty Buttery Crepes, 55

pretzels, Pillowy Soft Cinnamon Sugar Pretzels,
122–3
profiteroles, *Pâte à Choux* Dough, 29, 38–9, 82
puff pastry
about, 12
baking techniques, 23
caramelizing, 23, 34
double fold/single fold, 207
Mini Almond Puff Pastry Raspberry Boats, 167
Mini Apple Turnovers, 164
Mini Palmier Hearts, 96–7
Mini Swiss Pastries, 166
My Famous Tarte Tatin, 148–9
Rough Puff Pastry, 33–4, 154, 164, 167
XL Queen of Hearts, 154

Q

Quiche Dough, 37

R

raspberries
Mini Almond Puff Pastry Raspberry Boats, 167
Raspberry Blossom Almond Cake Bites, 76–7
Raspberry Cinnamon Nonnettes, 85
Rich and Fluffy Chocolate Cake with Magic
Mascarpone Mousse and Marinated
Berries, 180–1
rocher topping, 113
Rough Puff Pastry, 33–4, 96, 154, 164, 167
royal icing, 158
Rum Nantes Cake, 176

S

sable dough, 32, 36, 70
sauces
for Churro Bites, 147
Crème Anglaise, 42
Thick Salted Butter Caramel Sauce, 58
scones, Coconut Scone Brunch Bites, 78
sheet cake, 115
simple syrup, 61
single fold, puff pastry, 207
Smores Cookie Pizza, 138
snack mix, Pantry Chocolaty Snack Mix, 168
Soft and Chewy Sugar Cookies, 40
Soft as Cotton Cheesecake, 128–9
soufflés, Chocolate Soufflés, 188
spiced syrup, 61
spreads
Hazelnut Praline Paste, 53
Homemade Hazelnut Chocolate Spread, 52
See also fillings
strawberries
Fresh Strawberry Tart, 153
strawberry shortcake, 141
XL Fresh Strawberry Choux to Share, 161
sugar
age of, 12
brown sugar, 14
caramel, 57
conversion chart, 208
inverted sugar, 24, 57
meringue baking techniques, 24–5
pearl sugar, 82
powdered sugar, 14
simple syrup, 61, 134, 135
storing, 14
vanilla sugar, 18

Sugar Cookies, 40
sweet chestnut cream, Chocolate Fondant Cake
Bites, 81
Sweet Pastry Dough, 32
Swiss meringue, 24
Swiss Meringue Buttercream, 47
Swiss Rochers, 175
Swiss Roll, 126–7

T

tart shells, 36, 37
tarts
Fresh Strawberry Tart, 153
Giant Frosted Choco Tart, 158
My Famous Tarte Tatin, 148–9
Pear Almond Galette, 150
tempering
chocolate, 26
egg yolk mixture, 42, 43, 44
Thick and Chewy Chocolate Chip Cookies, 201
Thick Salted Butter Caramel Sauce, 58
truffles, Creamy Chocolate Truffles, 173
turnovers, Mini Apple Turnovers, 164

U

unsalted butter, 26

V

vanilla
about, 13, 15
Almond Cream, 49
Crème Anglaise, 42, 43
Pastry Cream, 29, 44, 153
scraping vanilla beans, 60
vanilla bean powder, 15
vanilla butter, 14
vanilla extract, 15
vanilla sugar, 15
volume measurement equivalents, 209

W

Waffle Sticks with Maple Butter, 104
weight measurement equivalents, 209
Wet Caramel, 57
whipped butters, 14
whole egg foam batter, 22
windowpane test, 25

X

XL Fresh Strawberry Choux to Share, 161
XL Queen of Hearts, 154

Y

yeast
autolyzing, 12, 25
testing before using, 25
types, 12
yogurt, Fresh Yogurt Cake, 197

weldon**owen**

an imprint of Insight Editions
P.O. Box 3088
San Rafael, CA 94912
www.weldonowen.com

CEO Raoul Goff
VP Publisher Roger Shaw
Editorial Director Katie Killebrew
Senior Editor Karyn Gerhard
Editorial Assistant Jon Ellis
Art Director Allister Fein
VP Manufacturing Alix Nicholaeff
Senior Production Manager Joshua Smith
Senior Production Manager, Subsidiary Rights Lina s Palma-Temena

Weldon Owen would also like to thank Karen Levy,
Janet Perlman, and Margaret Parrish for their extraordinary
work on this book.

Photography by Amanda Loren

ISBN: 979-8-88674-117-9

Manufactured in China by Insight Editions
10 9 8 7 6 5 4 3 2 1

ROOTS of PEACE   REPLANTED PAPER

Insight Editions, in association with Roots of Peace, will plant two trees for each tree
used in the manufacturing of this book. Roots of Peace is an internationally renowned
humanitarian organization dedicated to eradicating land mines worldwide and convert-
ing war-torn lands into productive farms and wildlife habitats. Roots of Peace will plant
two million fruit and nut trees in Afghanistan and provide farmers there with the skills
and support necessary for sustainable land use.

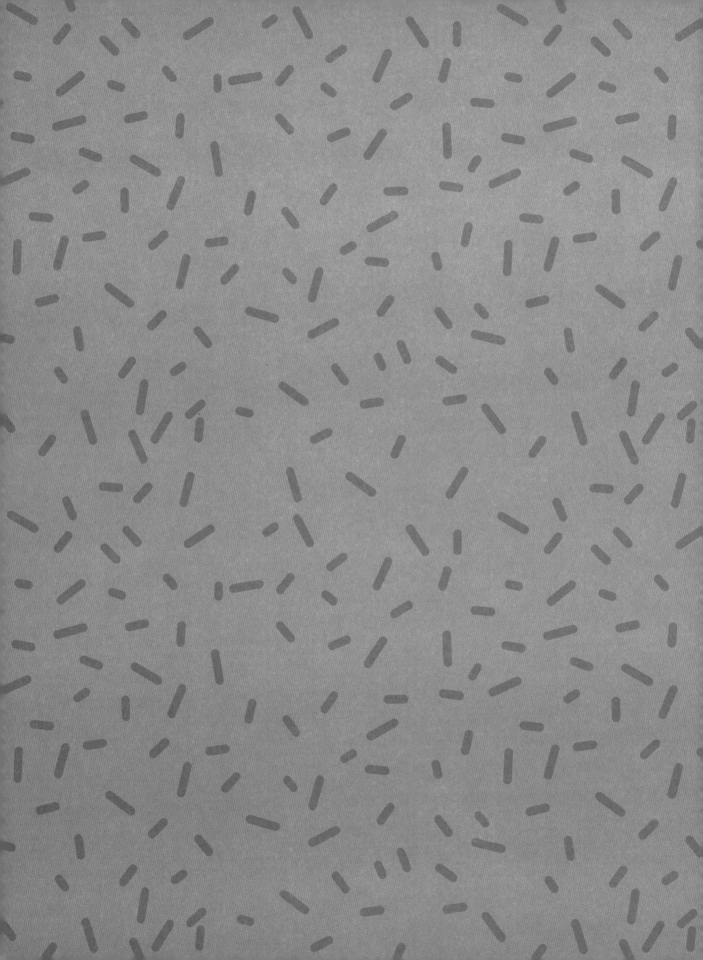